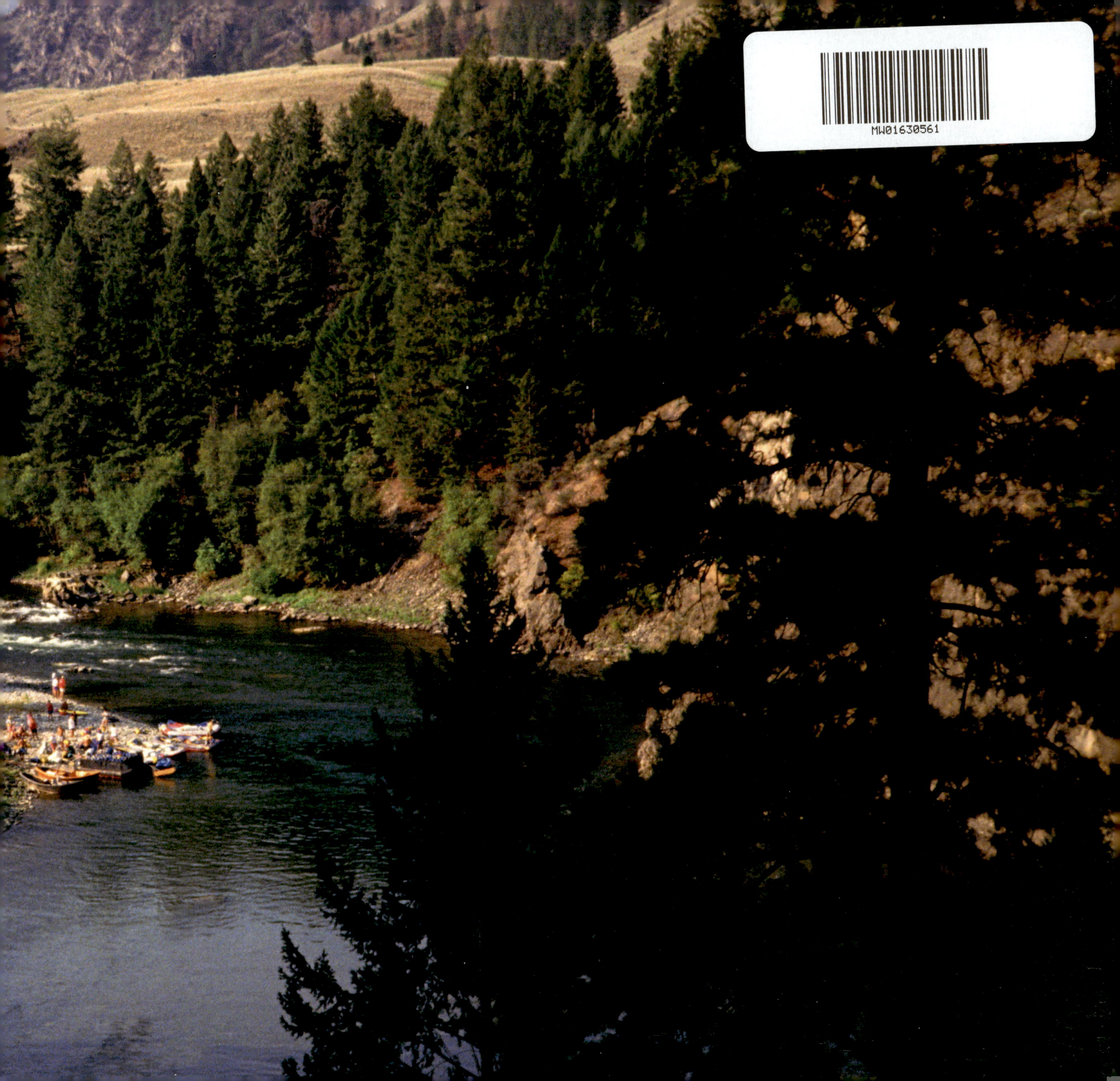

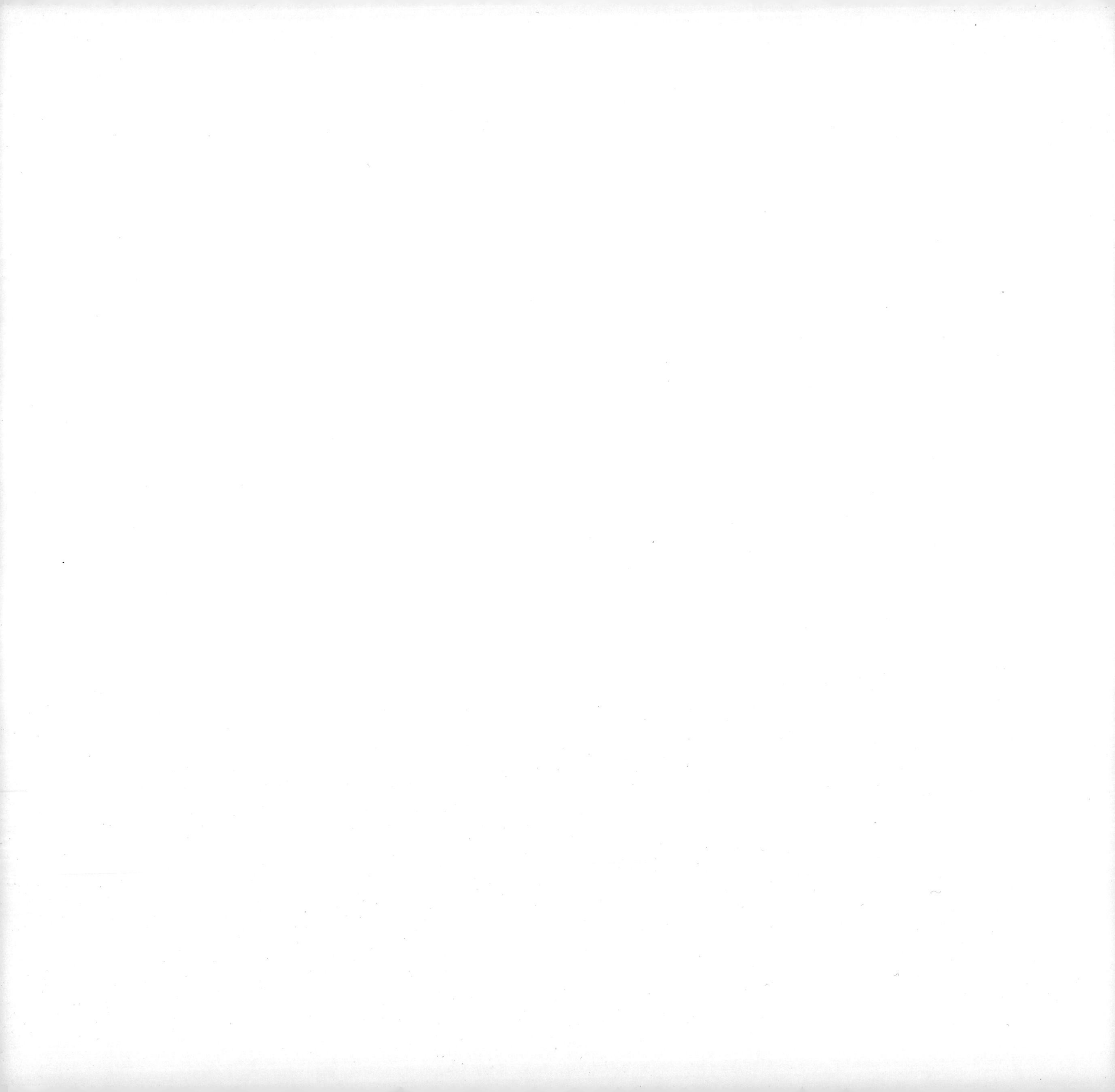

Reflections of the Middle Fork of the Salmon

A Visual Essay of America's Premier Wilderness River

by Bruce Bischof

Visual creation by Dan Armstrong & Russ Fry
Previous spread: Wollard Creek Camp (Mile 75)

THE MIDDLE FORK OF THE SALMON

The Middle Fork of the Salmon is 100 miles of free-flowing river in the heart of the Frank Church – River of No Return Wilderness. Originating at the merging of Bear Valley and Marsh Creeks, it traverses northeast through the remote and rugged mountains of central Idaho. The Middle Fork of the Salmon was one of the original eight rivers nationally designated as Wild and Scenic on October 2, 1968. No road approaches the Middle Fork Canyon. Remote, isolate, but not desolate, the rugged landscape, crystal clear whitewater and extraordinary fishing of the Middle Fork of the Salmon are internationally recognized.

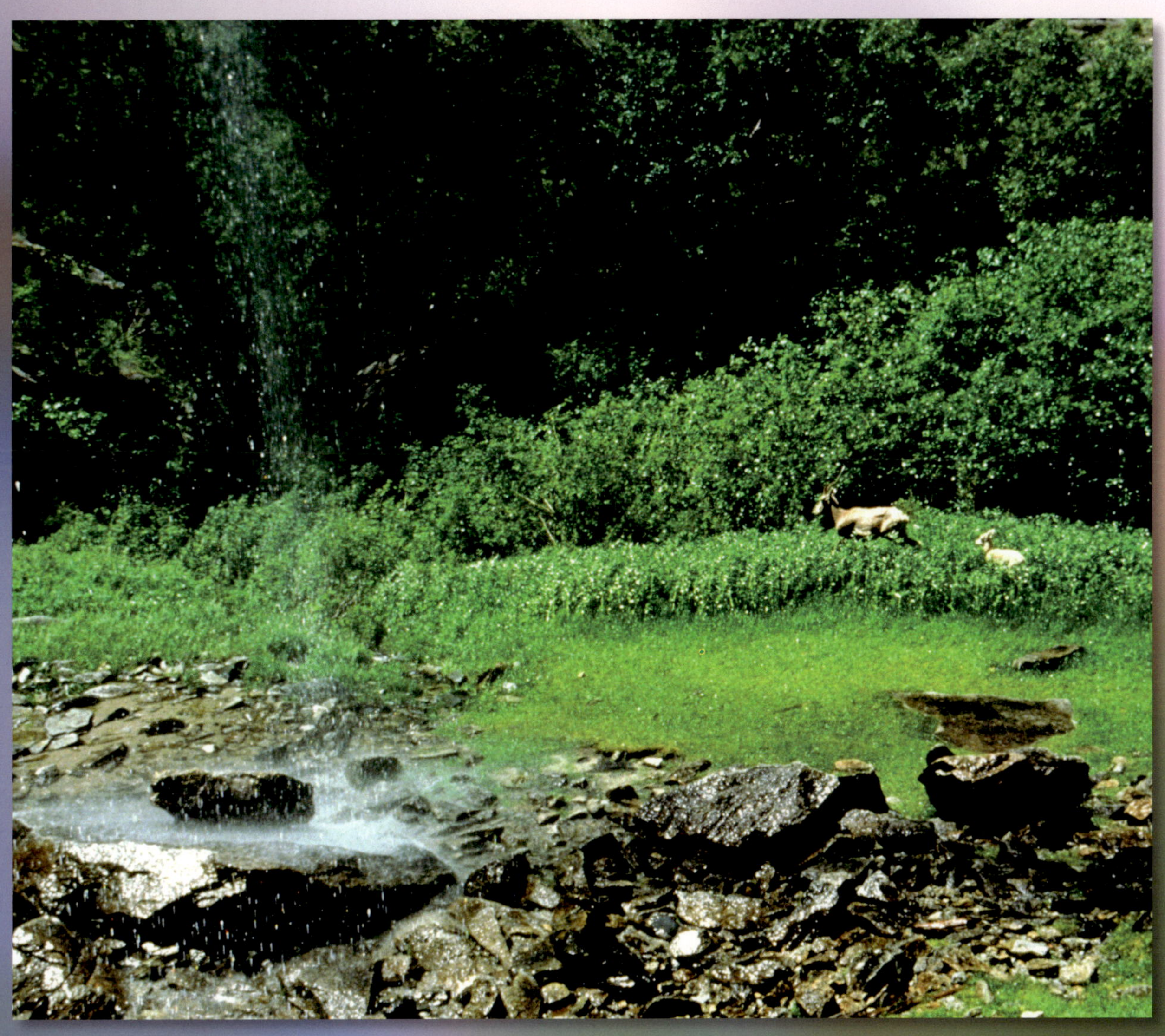

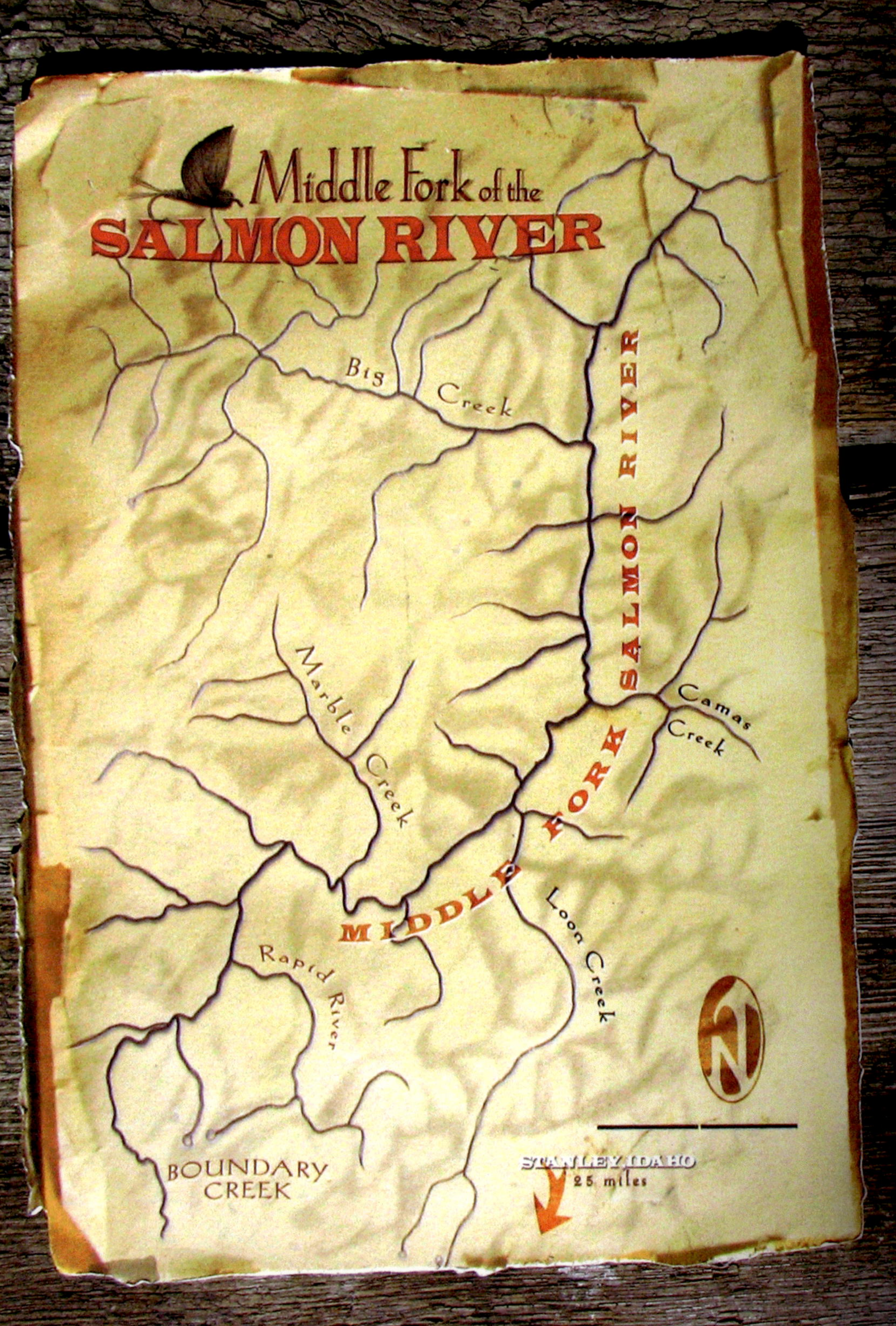

Caught on the Middle Fork

To cast a fly on a river you love
can right the world you live in.
To escape to waters that stir your soul
can cleanse the self with in.

Drifting a river with rod in hand,
employing one's fly casting skills,
holding on through waters white,
a marvelous blend of thrills.

Such can be found in a glorious place
at the nadir of a deep canyon,
where unspoiled nature demands attention,
on the Middle Fork of the Salmon.

The fish are there with blood red gills,
to be caught and released with a "thanks";
for the thrill of seeing it leap and run,
performing along bouldered banks.

A menu tied on their behalf
can be cast from a boat or in waders.
Royalty reigns with a Coachman or Wulf
or bodacious stimulators.

Few things in life spawn pleasant dreams
as does this drift of pleasure.
Beauty without becomes beauty within,
transformed by this natural treasure.

~ Dr. Bud Beamer

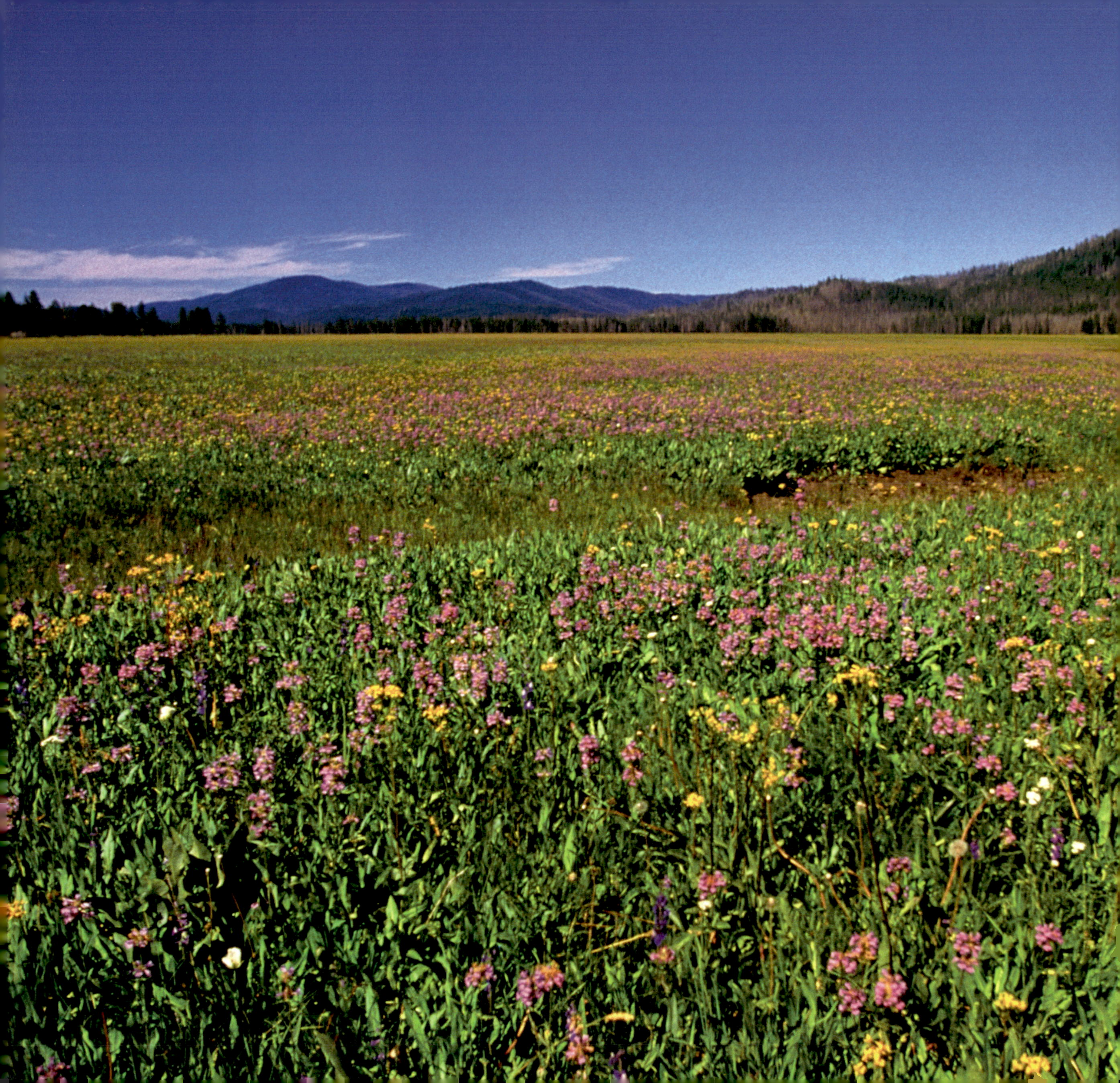

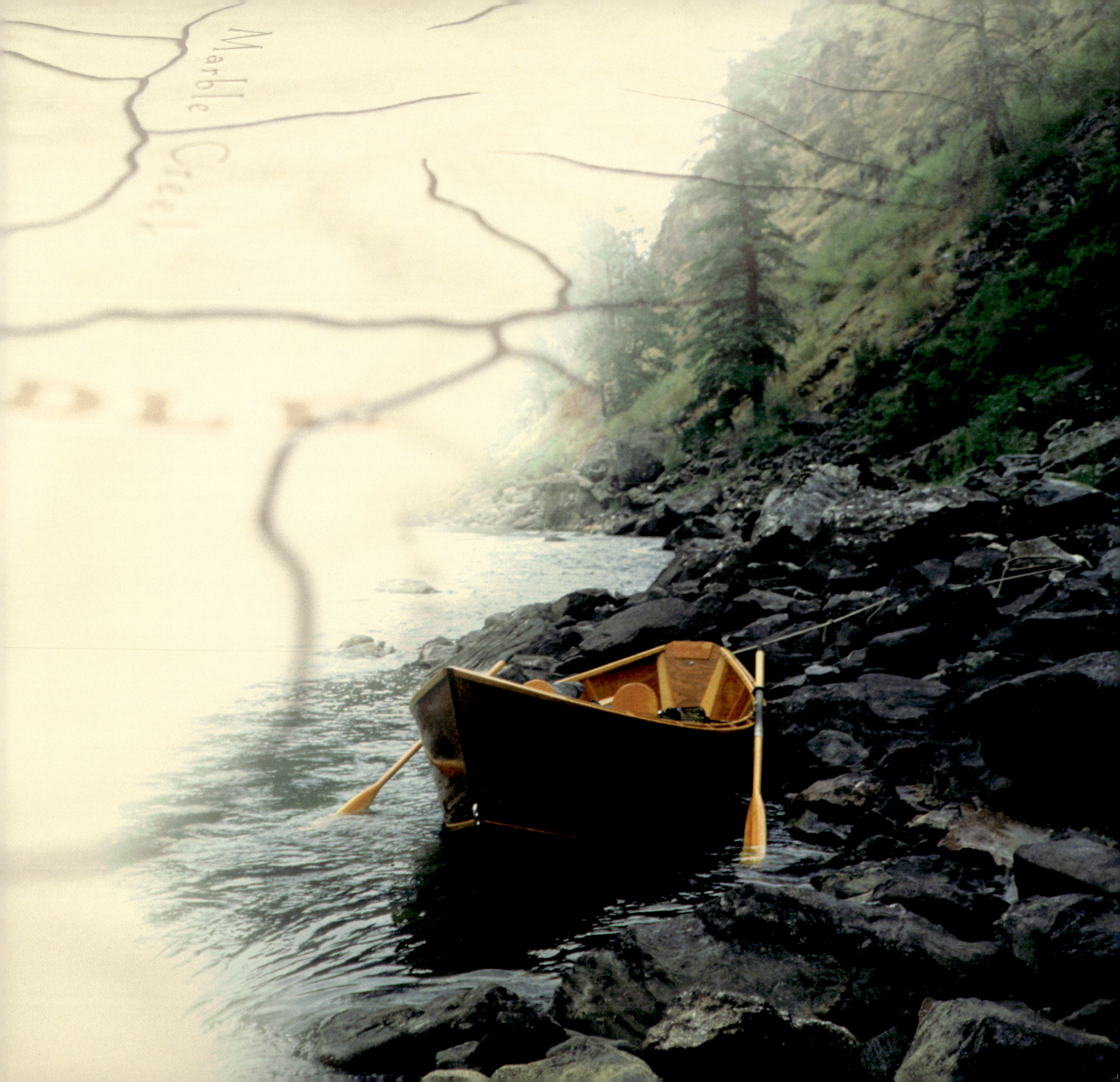
Marble

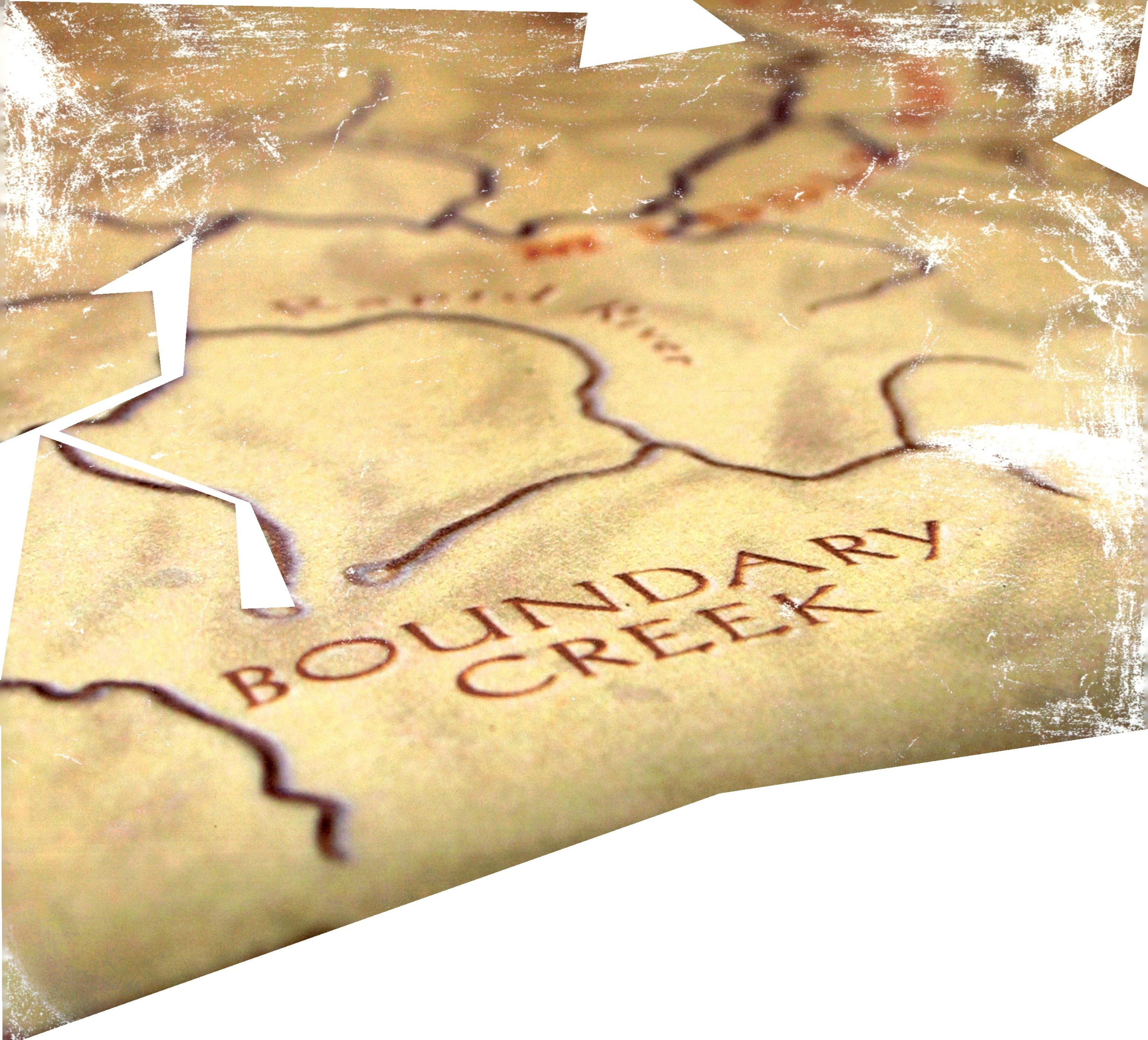
BOUNDARY CREEK

THE UPPER CANYON

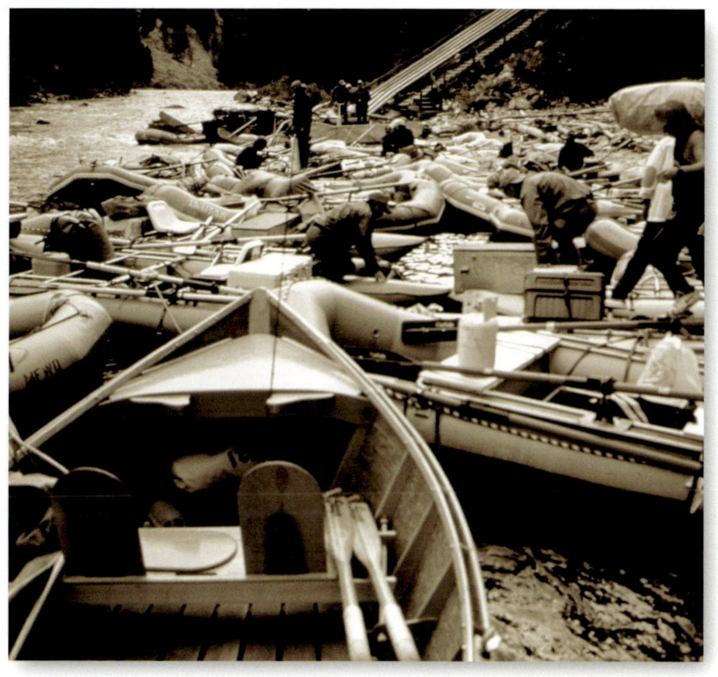

. . The upper canyon (mile 0–24) is a green, lush, high alpine forest speckled with a series of fast challenging rapids.

The upper river launch site is Boundary Creek located immediately below Dagger Falls. Progressing swiftly to Pistol Creek, the river then slows to Indian Creek (mile 25). The upper canyon is a lush, high alpine forest with a series of fast rapids. The put-in elevation is approximately 5,800 feet with an average river gradient of 28 feet per mile. Major rapids include Sulfer Slide, Ram's Horn, Velvet, The Chutes, Elk Horn, Power House, Artillery, Cannon Creek and Pistol. Sheepeater Hot Springs is located on the left side of the river (mile 12) and is considered one of the most popular campsites on the river. Deer, moose, and bear are regular visitors to the hot spring's beautiful, grassy, flats.

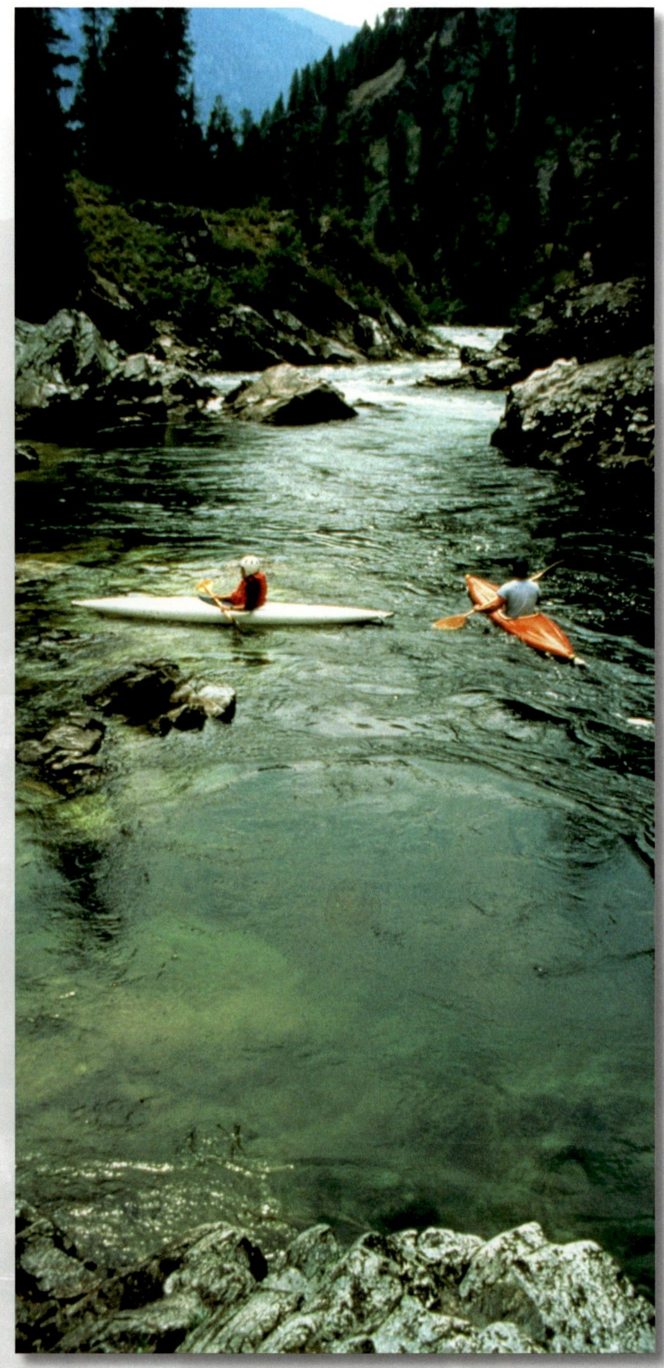

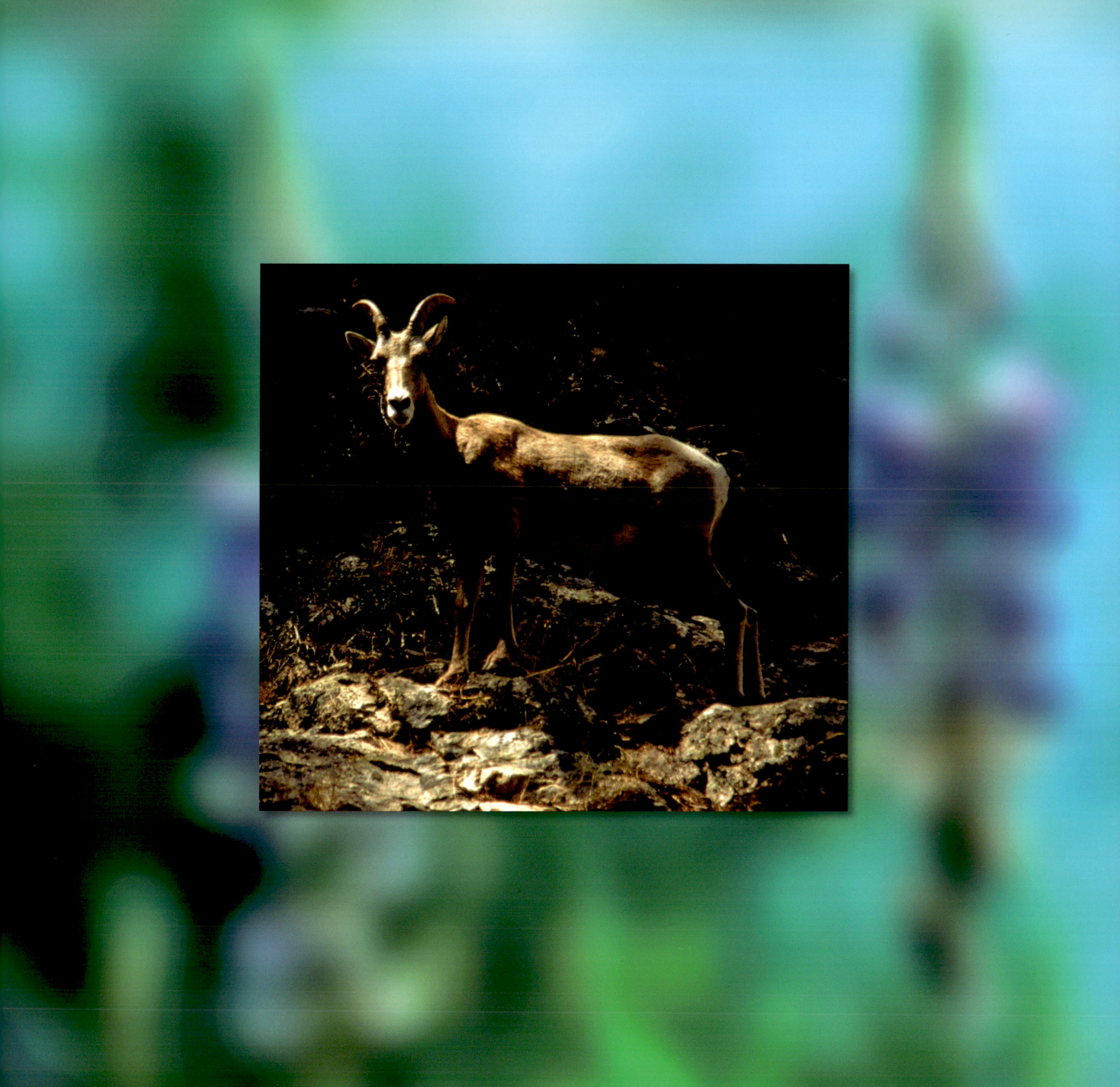

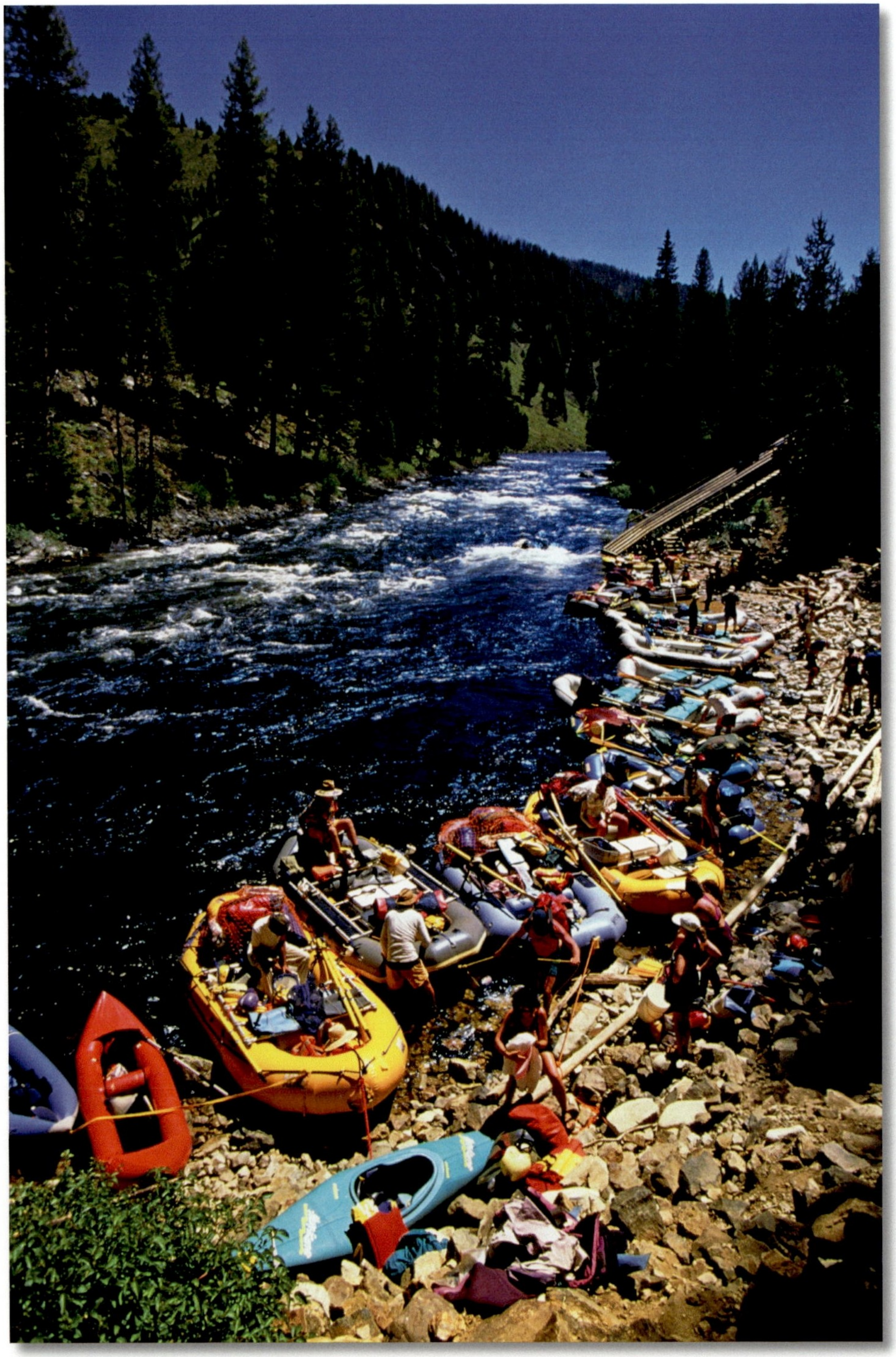

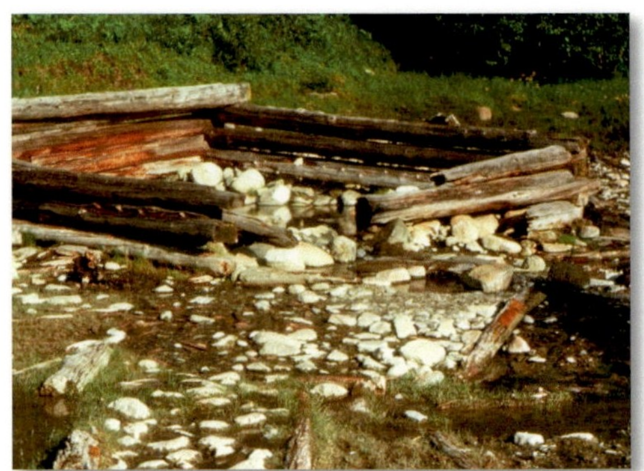

LEFT: Launch at Boundary Creek (mile 0)

TOP: Sheepeater Hot Springs (mile 12)

RIGHT: Paddle Boat Splishin' and Splashin'

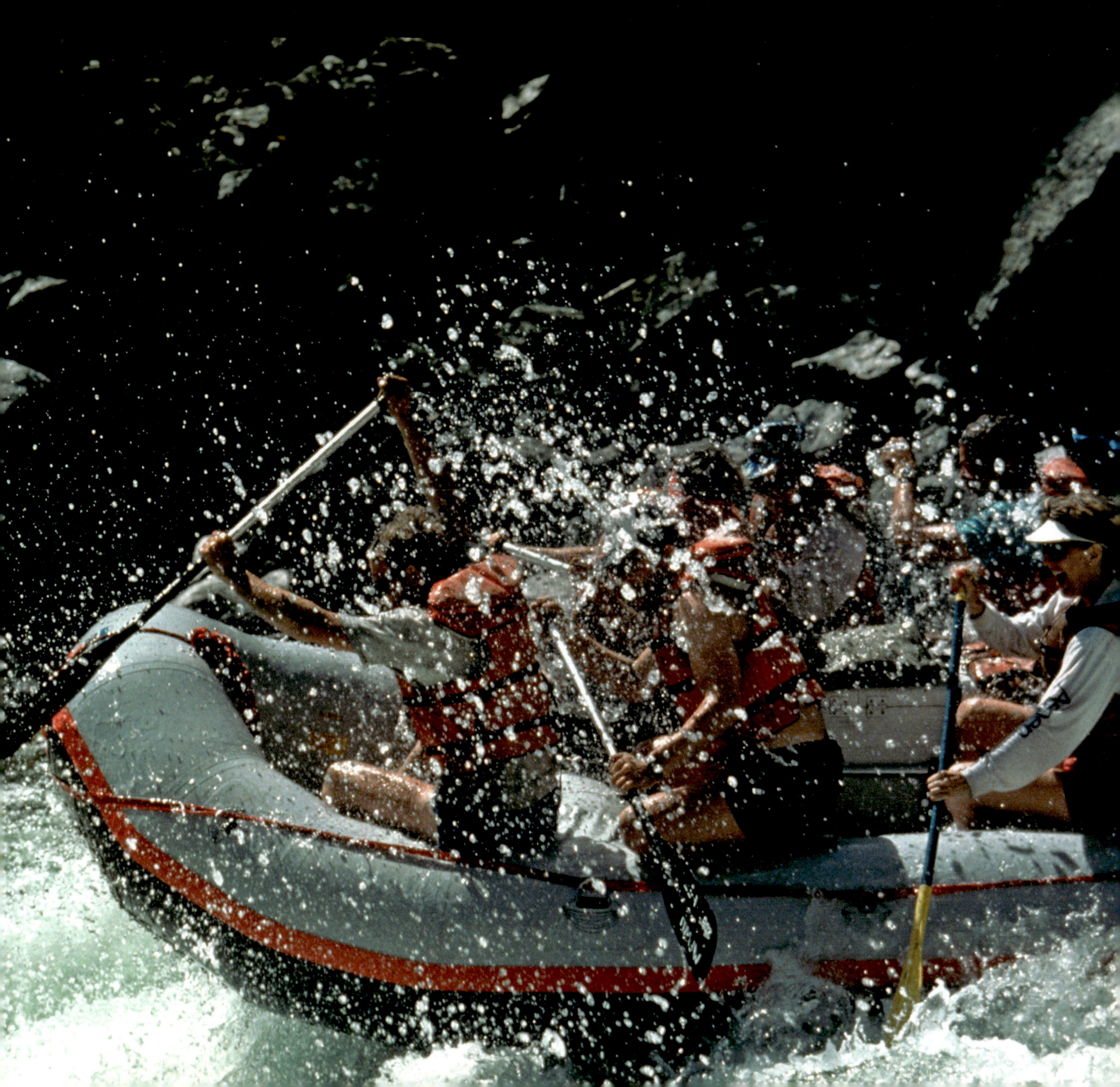

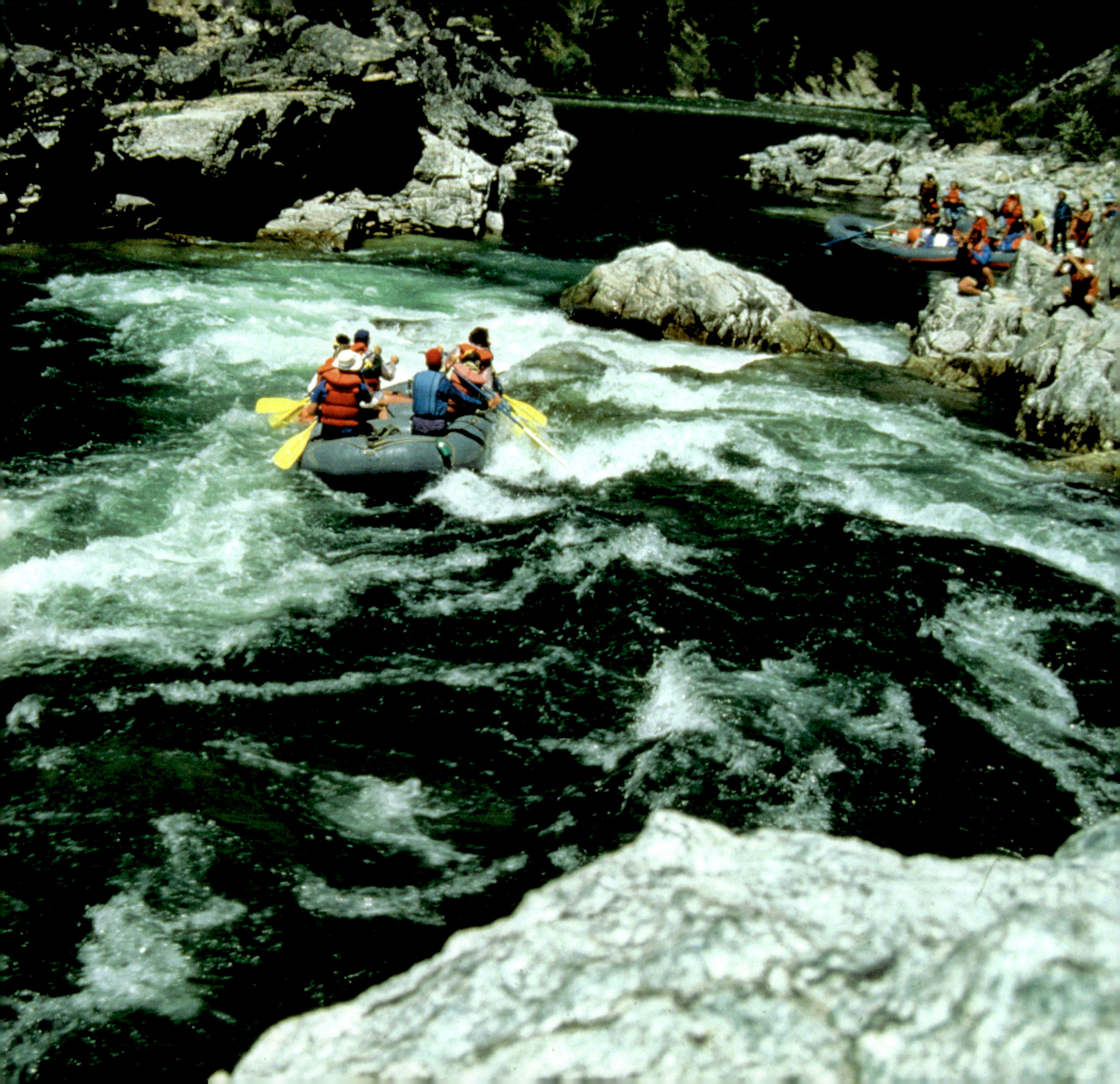

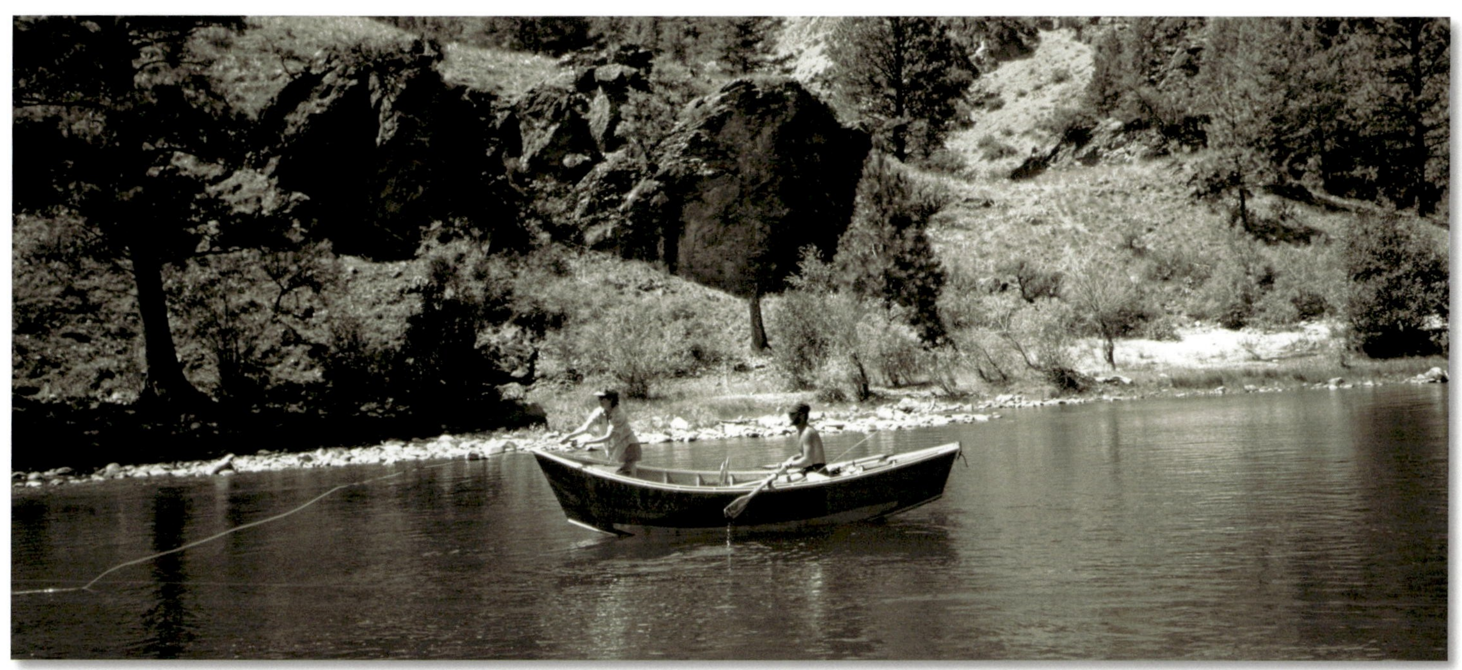

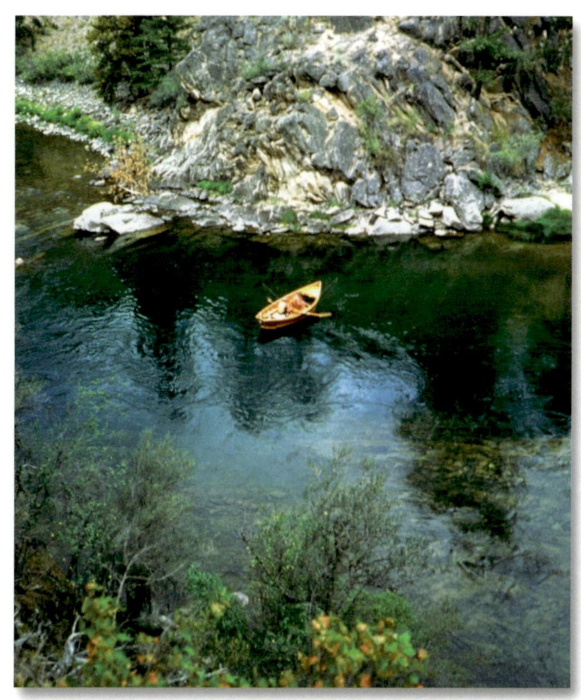

LEFT: Entering Pistol Creek Rapids (mile 21)

ABOVE & RIGHT: Expert boaters and fly fisherman opt for the float in wooden driftboats.

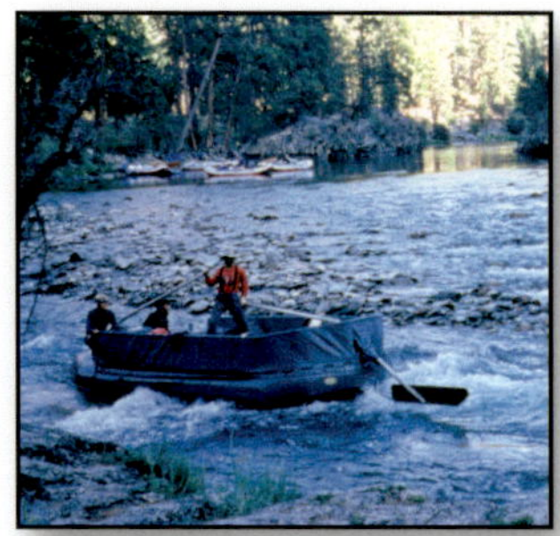

While many rivers have pool drops, a calm water stretch following a rapid, the Middle Fork of the Salmon remains flowing for the entire 100 miles, another one of its many unique attributes.

Early river transportation thus adopted this into boat construction that utilized the rivers current. Captain H. Guleke developed the sweep boat in the early 1900s to transport Salmon River pioneers, as well as goods and mining equipment, to places no other craft could access.

Sweep boat dimensions were roughly 30 feet long, 10 feet wide and 4 feet deep. The "sweeps" consisted of two poles, often made of peeled lodgepole pine trees, to which 12-foot blades were attached at the bow and the stern. Only needing to steer, not row the boat, it took one person to operate each sweep.

Today, operated by a single guide, the redesigned sweep boat has the capacity equivalent to three rafts. When the sweep boat leaves camp in the morning, there is no stopping until camp. The momentum of the river carries it, often making it to camp three to four hours before the rafts.

The skill to navigate a sweep boas is nearly a lost art, with only a handful of outfitters continuing to use them. They have become a legacy and a renowned river craft due to the fact they only operate on the Middle Fork of the Salmon in the entire world. No other river has the consistent flow to propel a craft of this size.

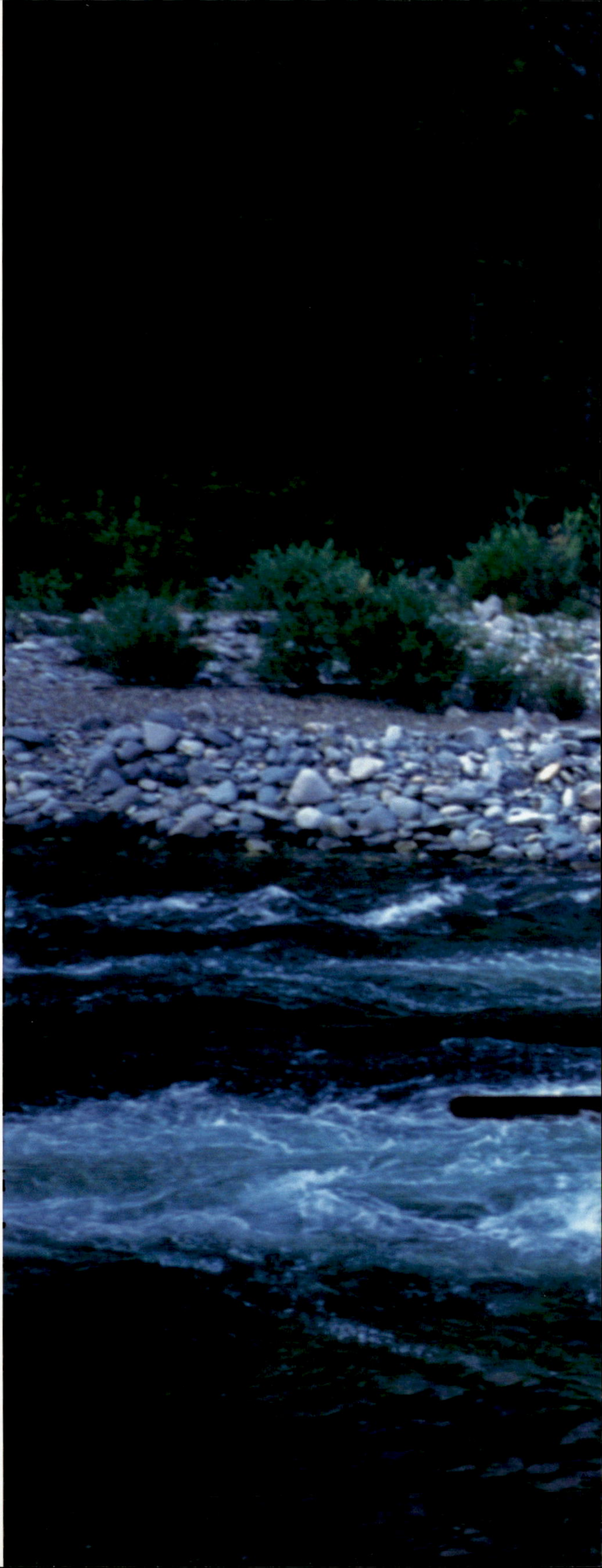

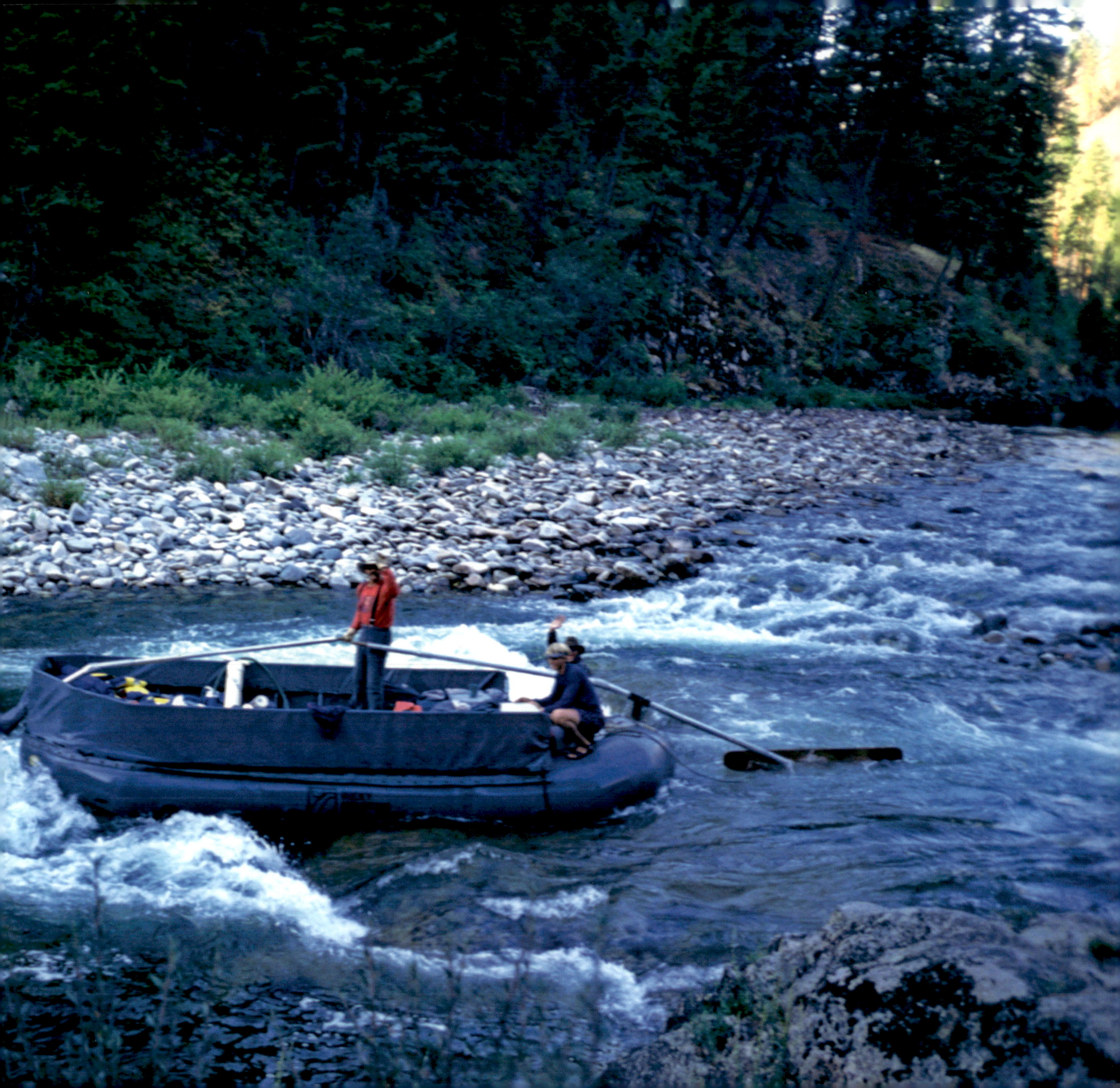

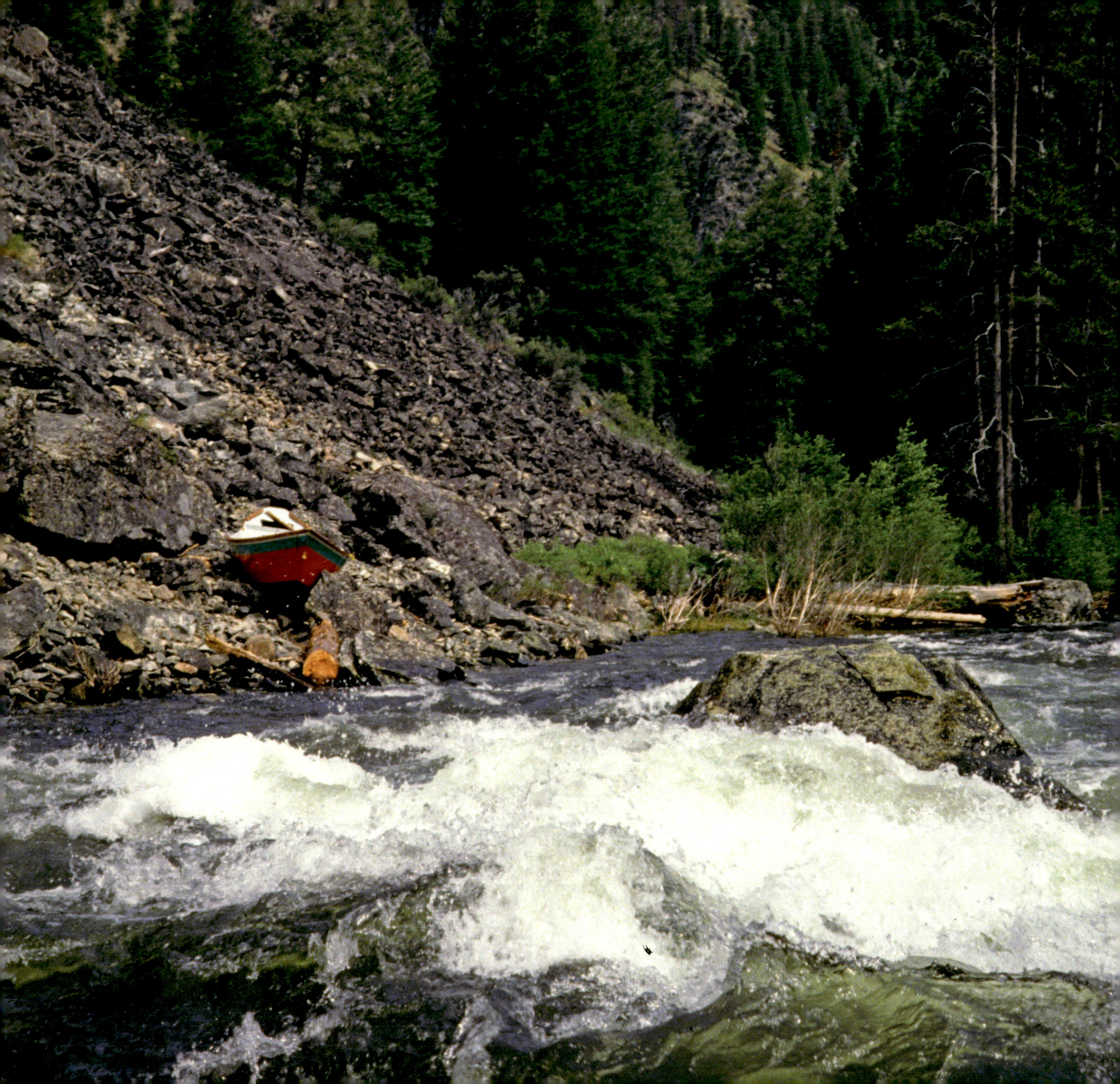

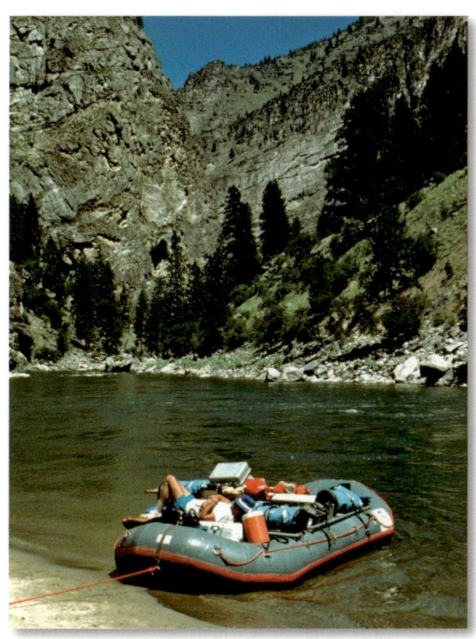

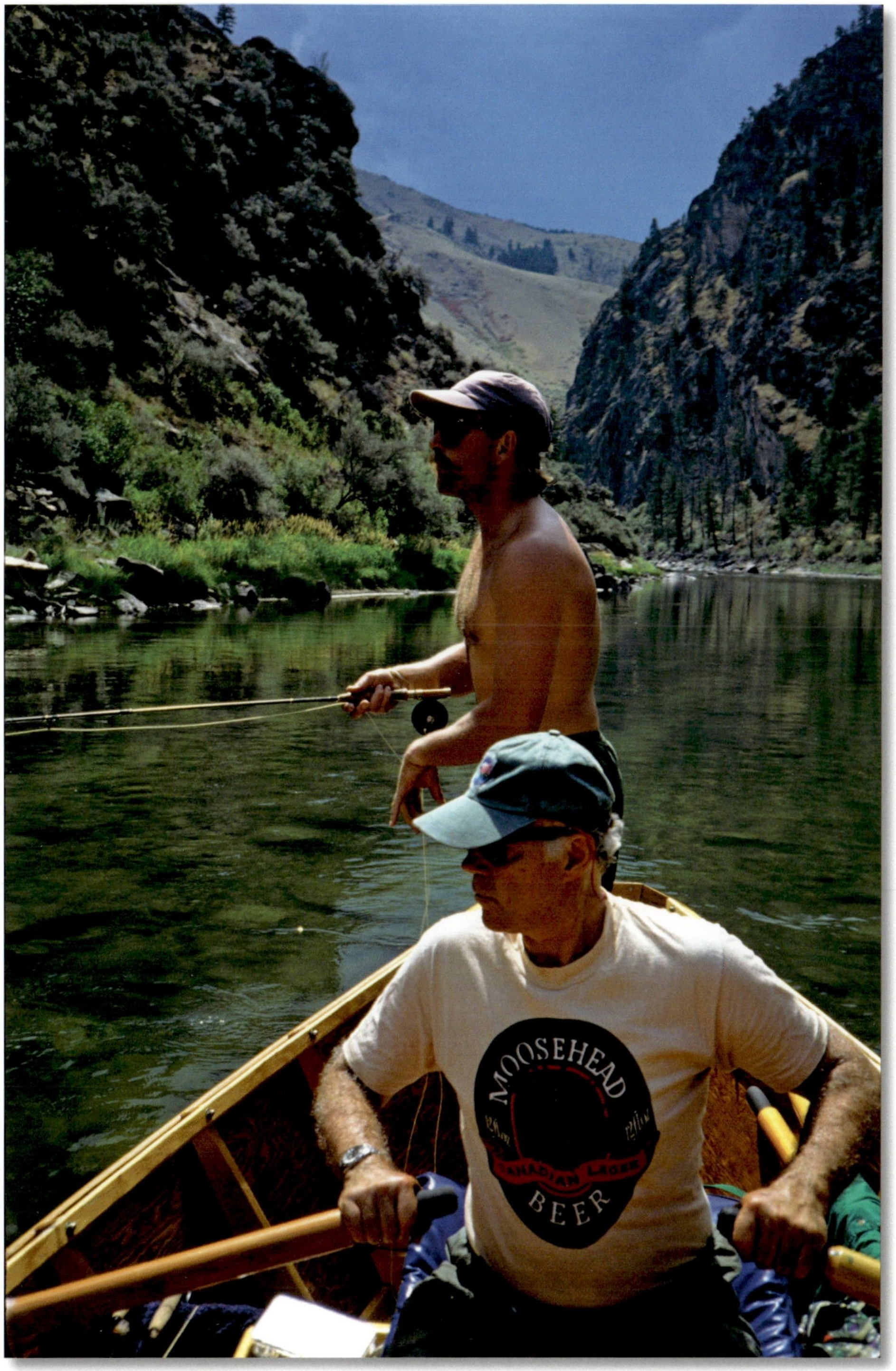

LEFT: Drift Boat High and Dry, Powerhouse Rapids (mile 11)

TOP: Catching Some Rays during an afternoon siesta

RIGHT: Author Bruce Bischof rowing veteran guide and friend, Eric Rector

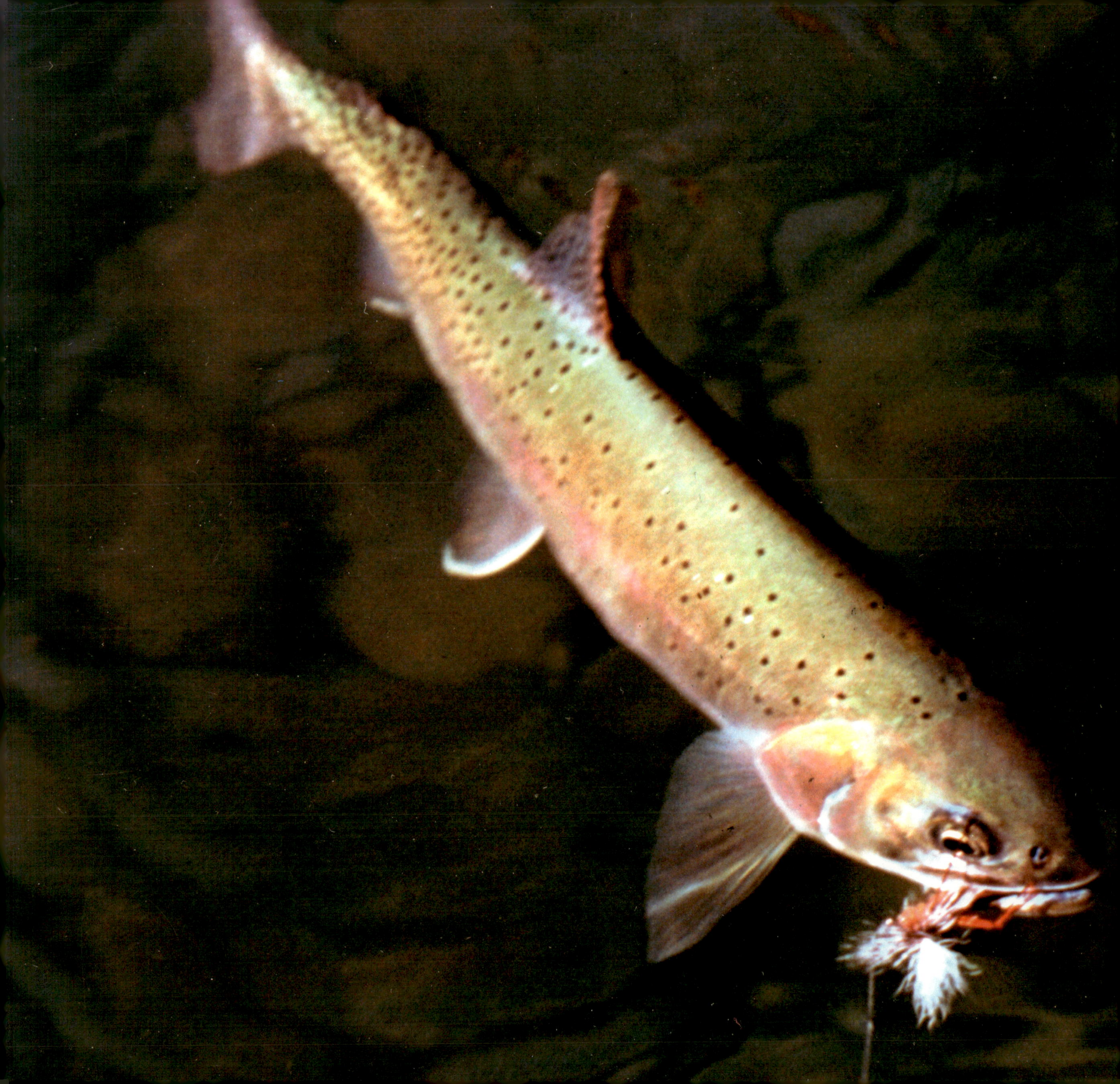

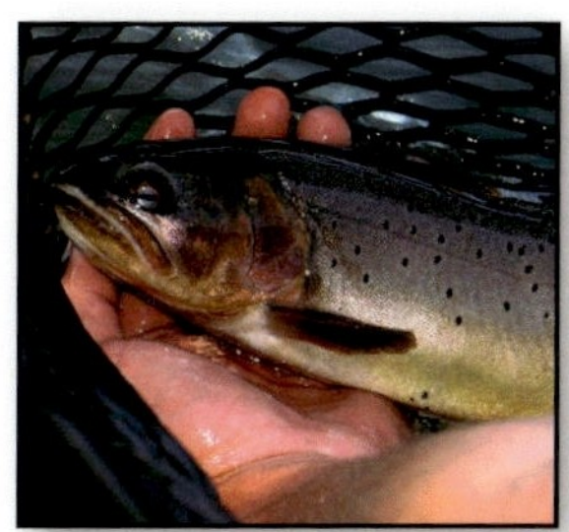

The Middle Fork is considered the finest dry fly west slope cutthroat fishery in North America. Prime fishing is typically late June through September with 100-fish days on dry flies not unusual. The average size is 12 inches with many fish running from 15 to occasionally 18 inches.

The fish hold in constant and predictable lies looking for aquatic insects. Most fishing is done from rafts or drift boats. An average angler will quickly learn to read the water locating fish immediately before or behind midstream rocks, current seams and adjacent to the river's banks.

Recommended flies are attractor patterns with the author's favorite being a Stimulator. Other popular flies include the Madam X, Hoppers, and Sofa Pillows. It is estimated that the Middle Fork holds approximately 3,000 fish per square mile with certain stretches exceeding 5,000. In recent years, the river is producing more rainbows. Catching several a day is not uncommon for anglers. Dolley Varden inhabit the deeper pools and are seldom caught on dries. All fishing is catch-and-release on barbless hooks.

A five-weight rod is typically used although a four-weight in non-windy conditions fished along the slower edge water may be preferable. Normal upstream afternoon winds in the middle and lower canyon may require a stronger rod. Due to the fast flows of the Middle Fork, 4X and 5X tippets on 10-foot leaders are recommended.

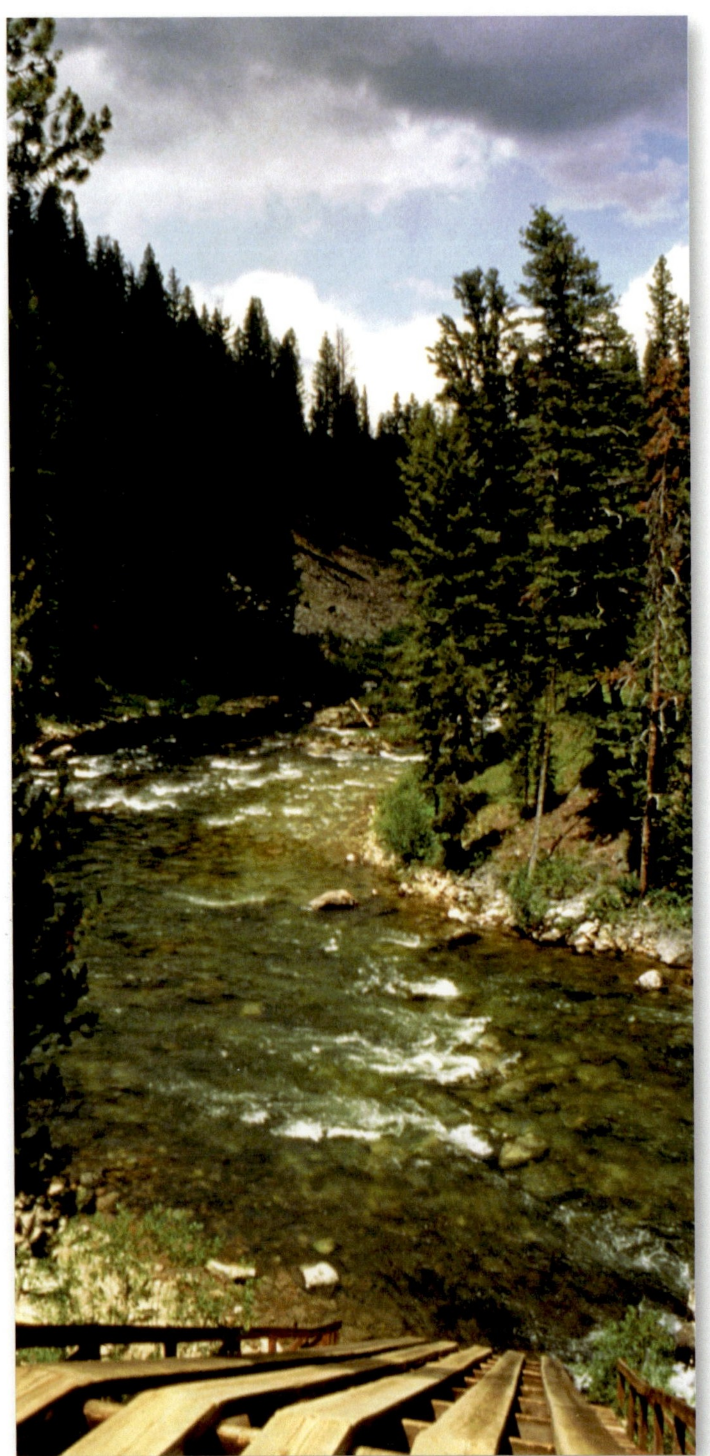

LEFT: Boat Ramp at Boundary Creek Launch (mile 0)

RIGHT: Author Bruce Bischof entering Velvet Falls with son Brandon (mile 5)

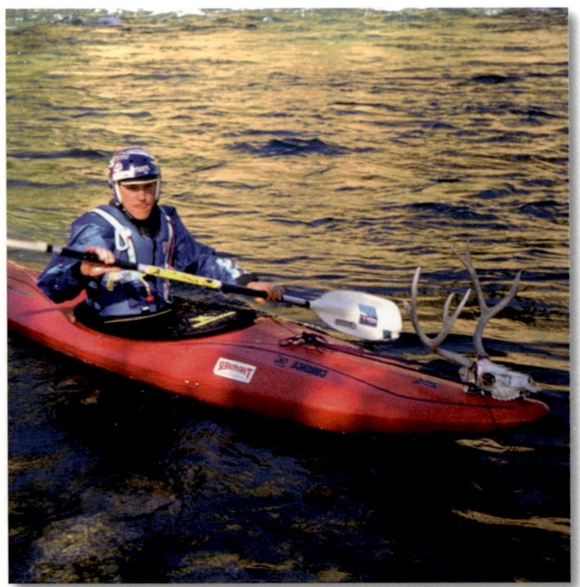

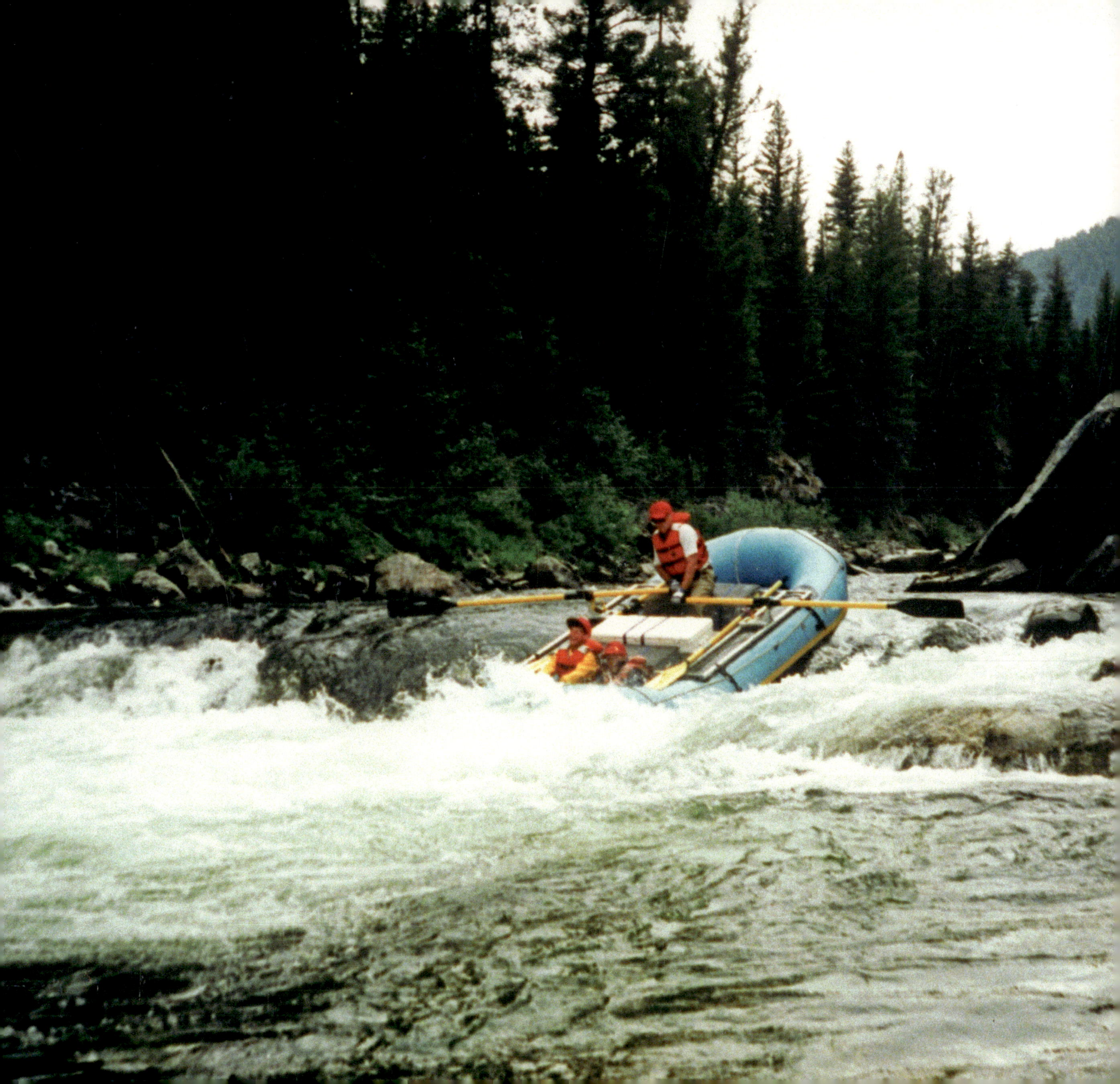

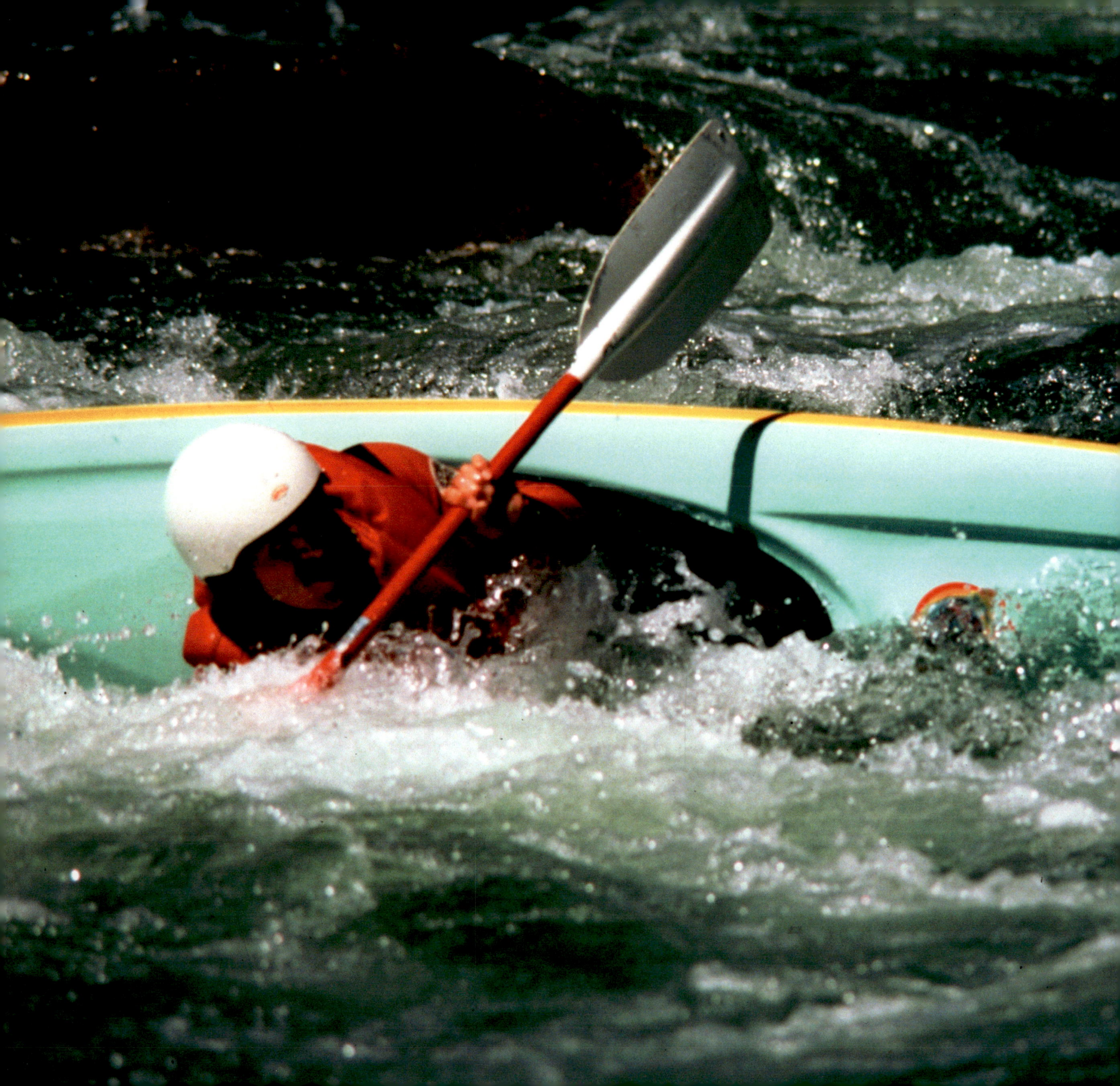

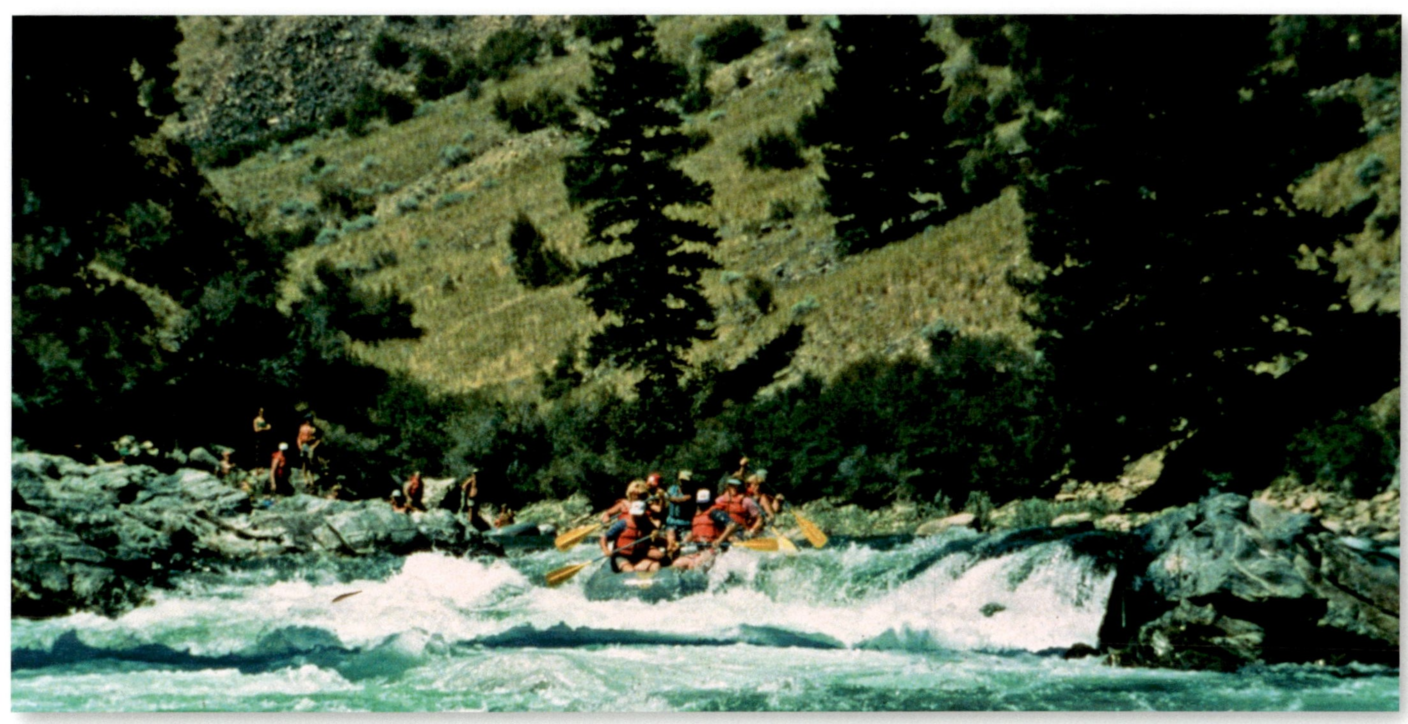

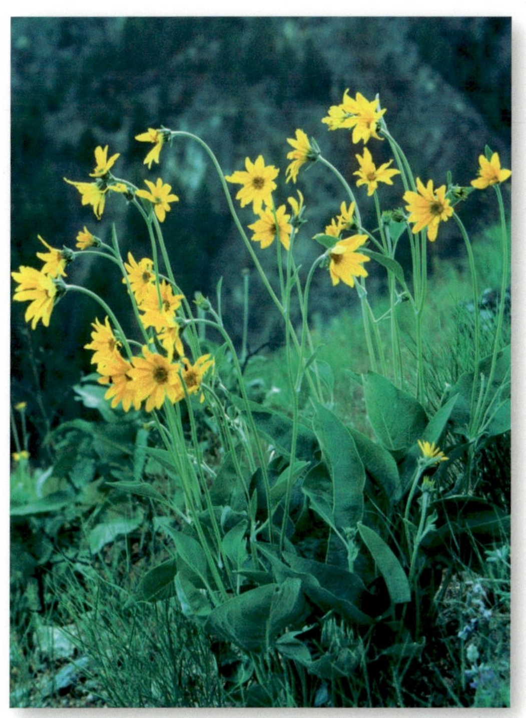

LEFT: A kayaker "Eskimo" rolling

ABOVE: Peanut Gallery on one of many rapids of the upper canyon

RIGHT: Wildflowers (these are from the Aster family) are abundant throughout the upper canyon

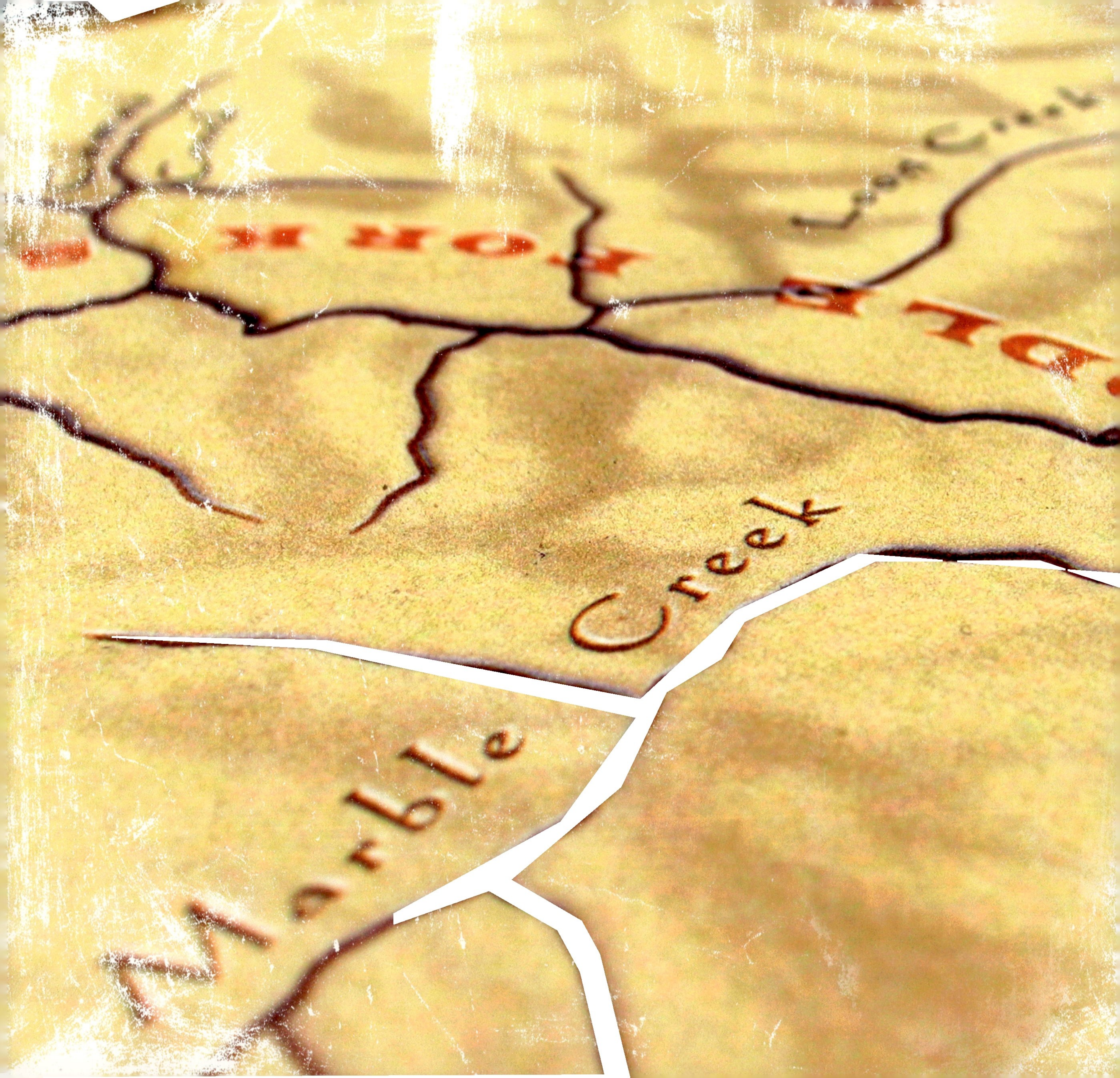
Marble Creek

THE MIDDLE CANYON

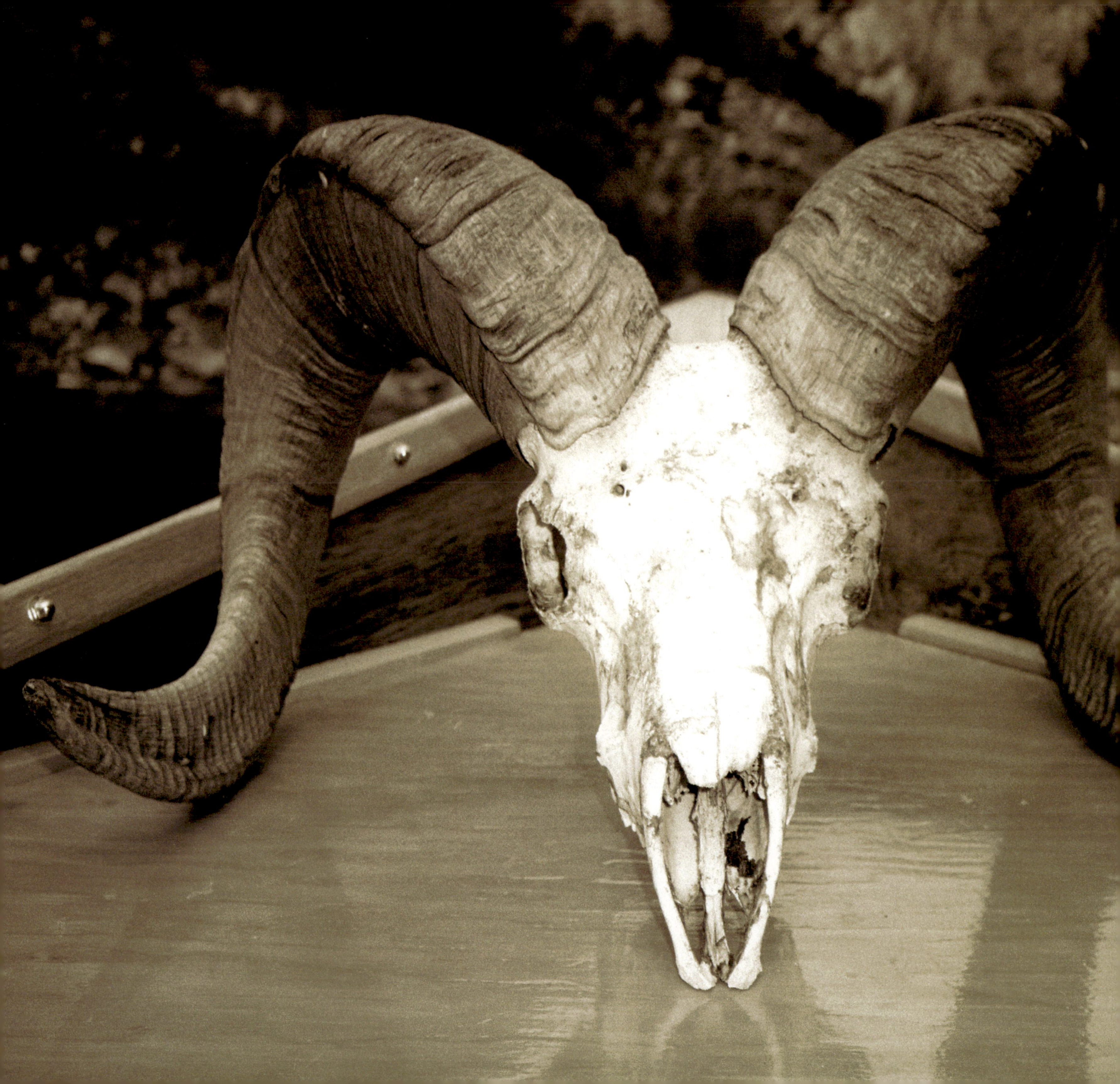

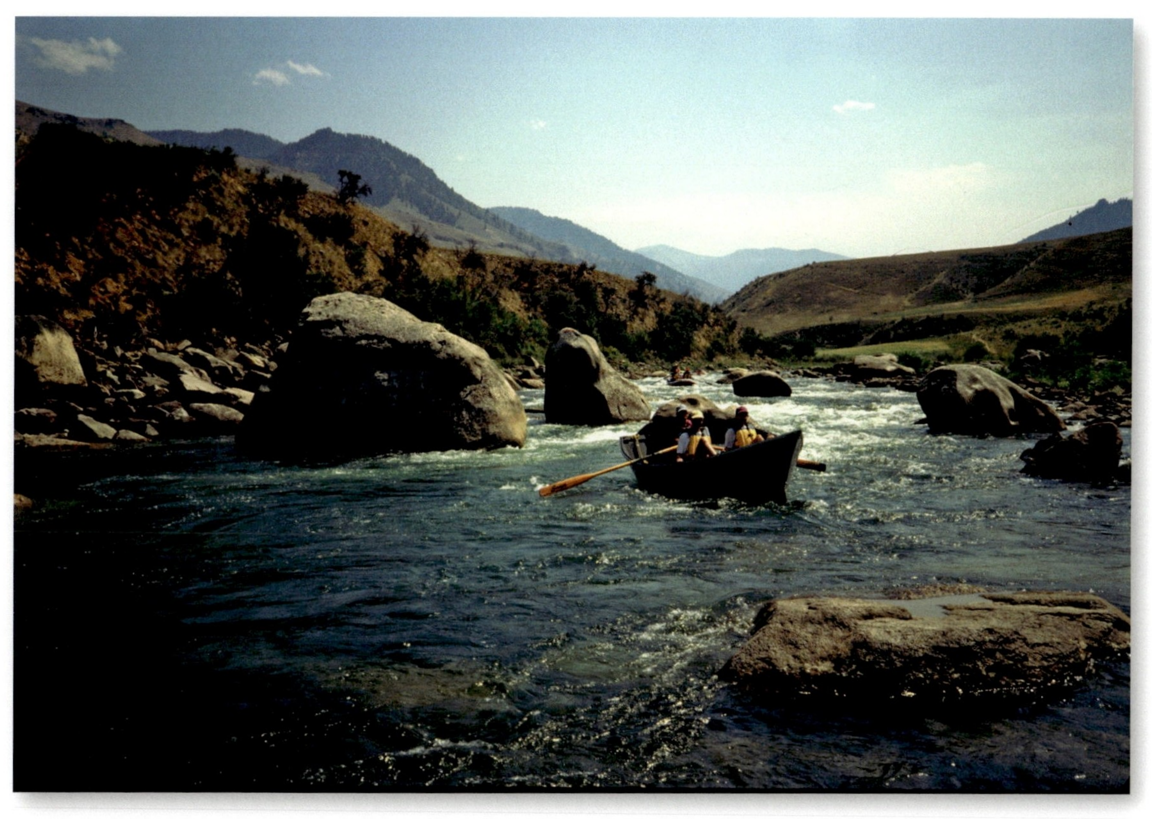

..The Middle Canyon (mile 25–68) changes from dense sub-alpine to Ponderosa Pine due to lower elevation and less moisture.

The Indian Creek Guard Station (mile 24) and camp is the second major launch site traditionally used when the water is too low to put in at Boundary Creek. Parties launching from Indian Creek will experience an unforgettable flight into the Forest Service Airstrip served by several backcountry air taxi services. From Indian Creek to Haystack Rapids (miles 24–68) the river slows with long stretches of relatively calm water laced with intermittent rapids. The canyon changes from dense sub-alpine to Ponderosa Pine due to lower elevation and less moisture. The middle canyon has eight major rapids including Oreo, Marble Creek, Jackass, the four Tappan rapids including Tappan Falls, and Aparejo Point. Several wonderful hot springs are found on the Middle Canyon including Sunflower Flats, Whitey Cox and Loon Creek. The Middle Fork Lodge (mile 33) and Hospital Bar (mile 52) holds the last hot springs camp on the river. The Tappan Ranch Cabin at Lower Grouse Creek Camp (mile 56) is a favorite campsite and was once visited by President Jimmy Carter. Approximately one mile down from the Tappan Ranch Cabin begins a series of rapids identified as Tappan 1, Tappan Falls, Tappan 2 and Tappan 3. The Tappan series of whitewater require expert boat handling with Tappan Falls being the largest drop on the river. A mile after Tappan rapids, Camas Creek (mile 60) enters the Middle Fork through a dramatic side canyon with a popular campsite at the mouth.

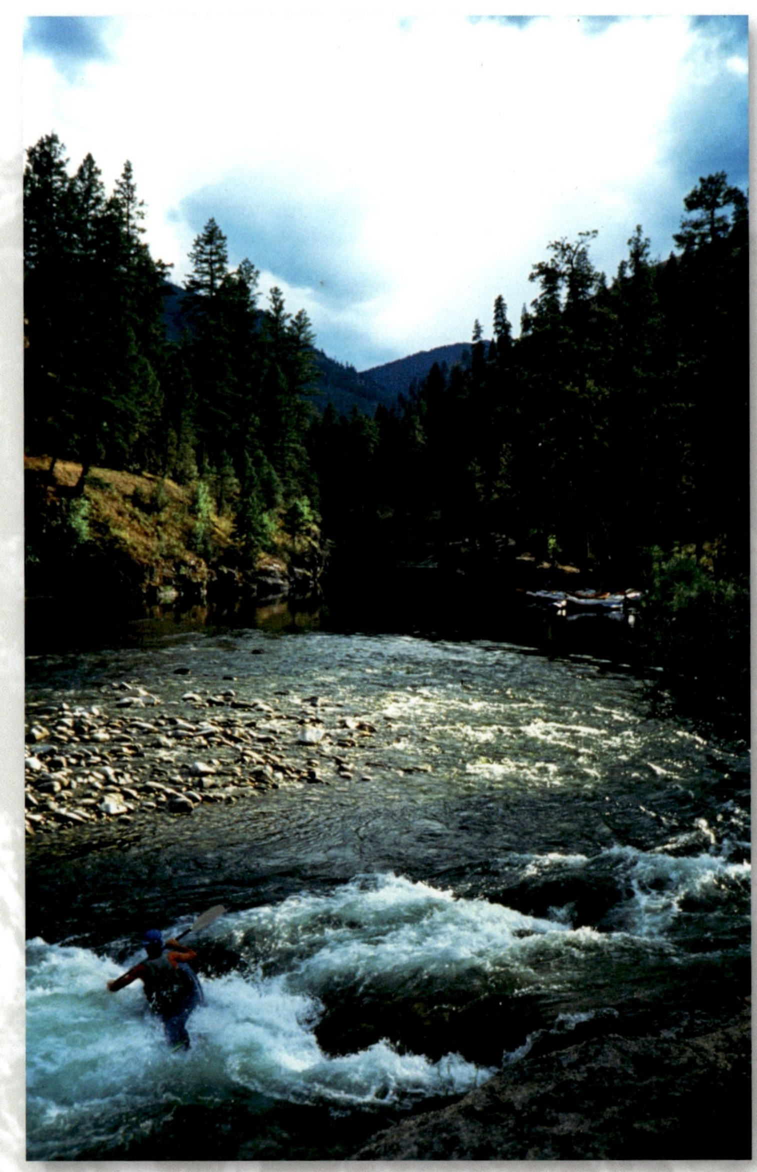

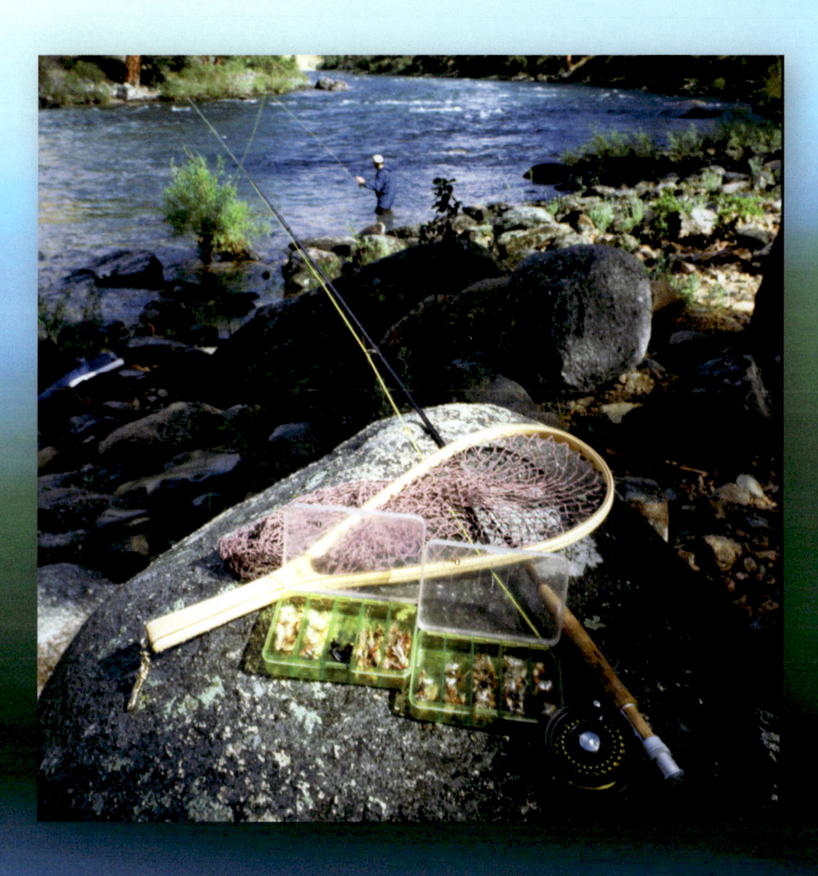

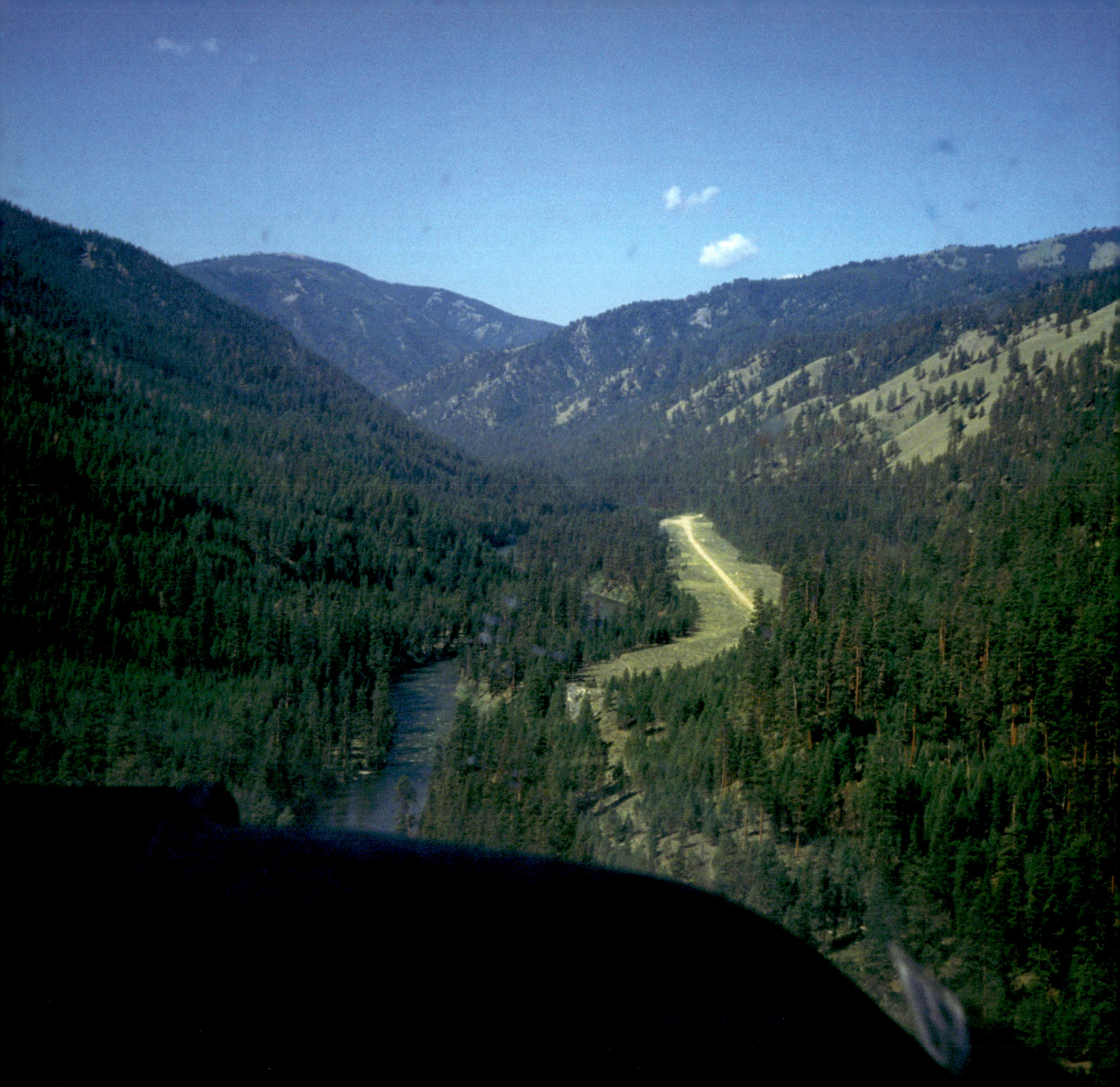

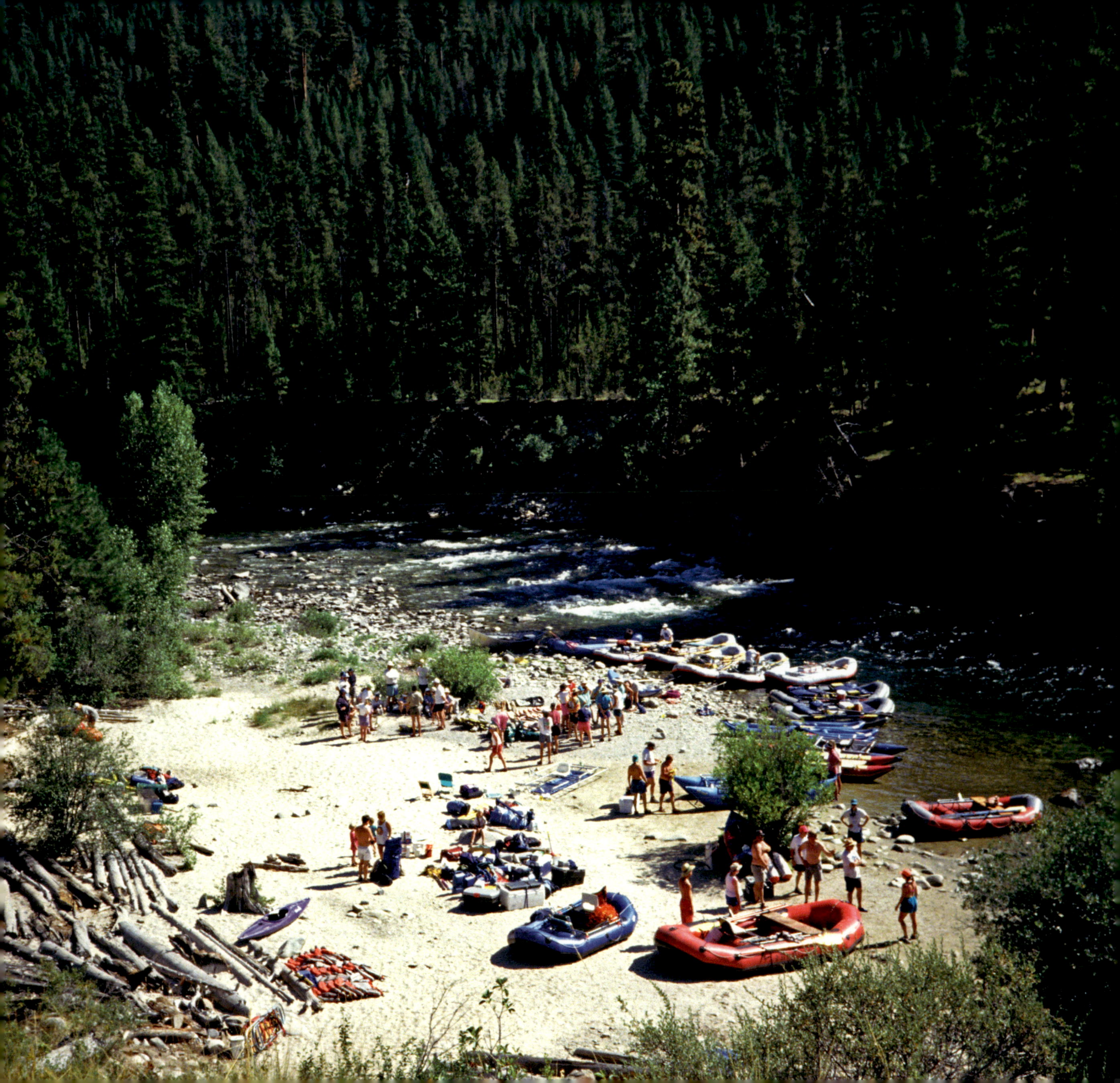

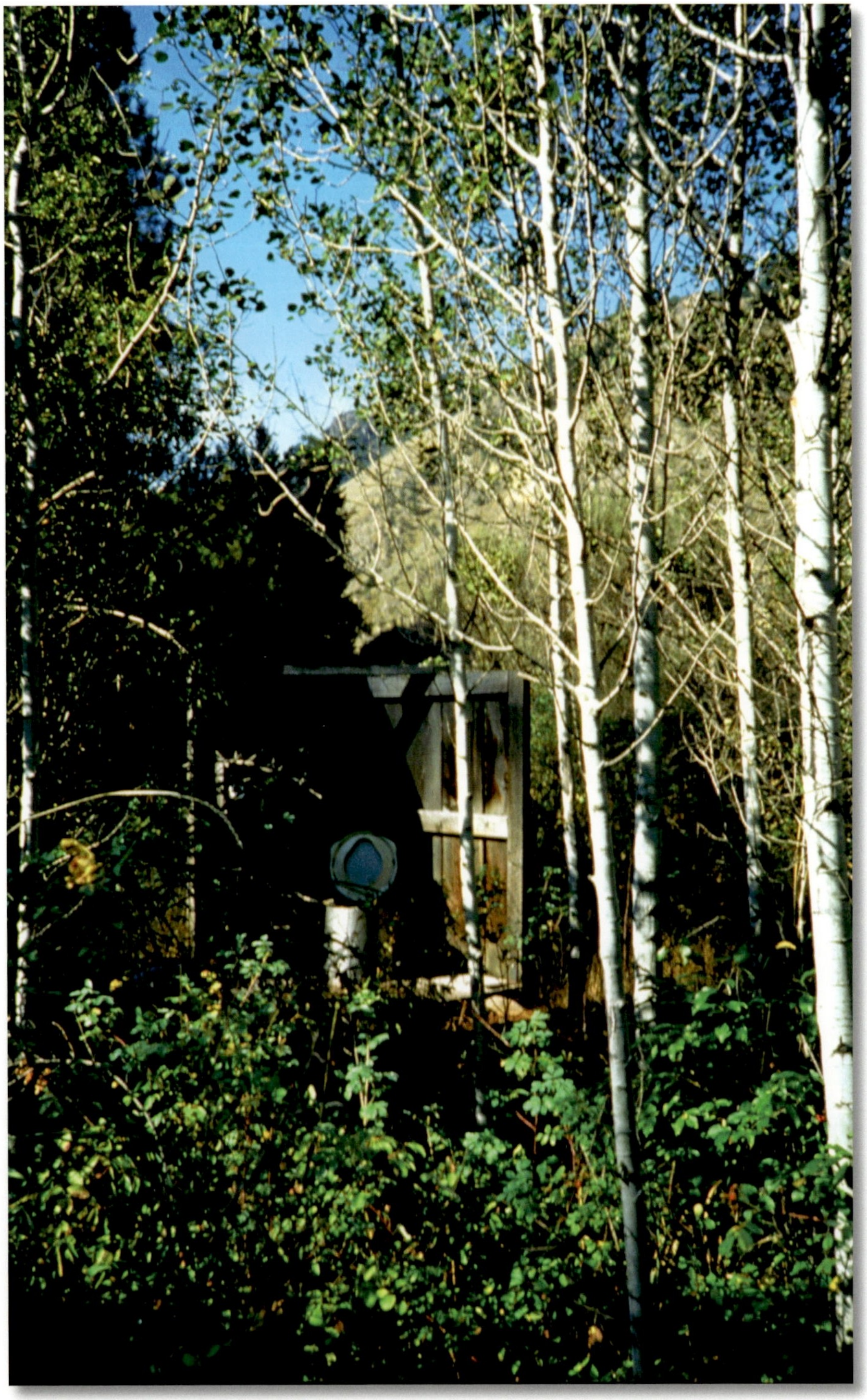

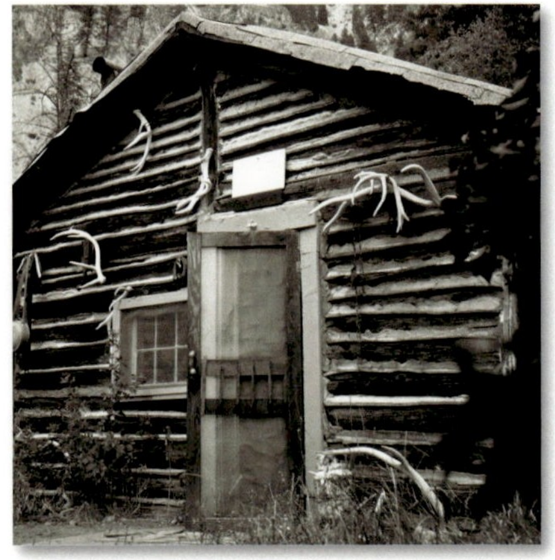

LEFT: "Growler" in the Aspens

ABOVE: Tappen Ranch Cabin

RIGHT: A kayaker bracing through a rapid in the Middle Canyon

PREVIOUS PAGES: Indian Creek air strip and launch site

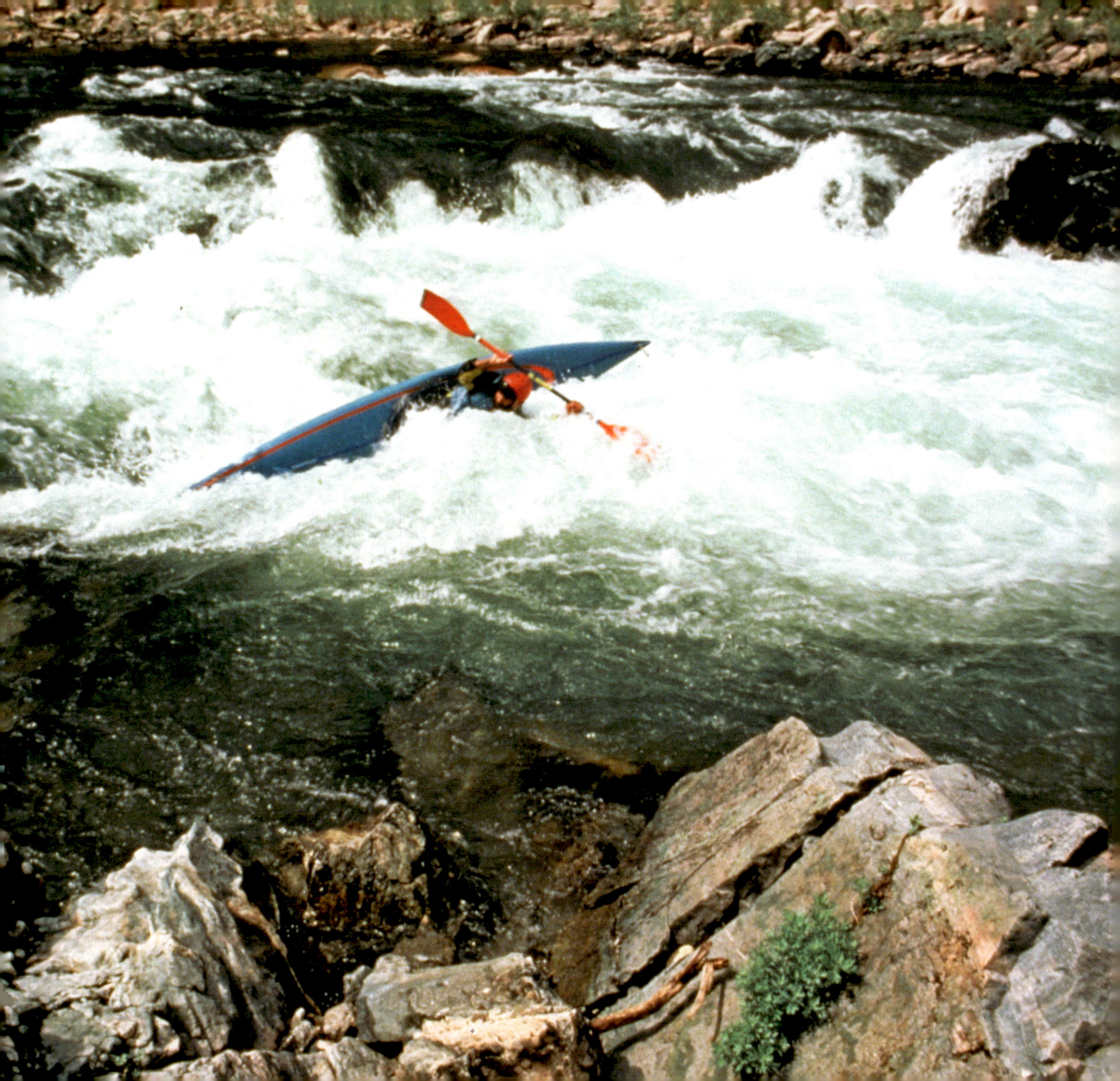

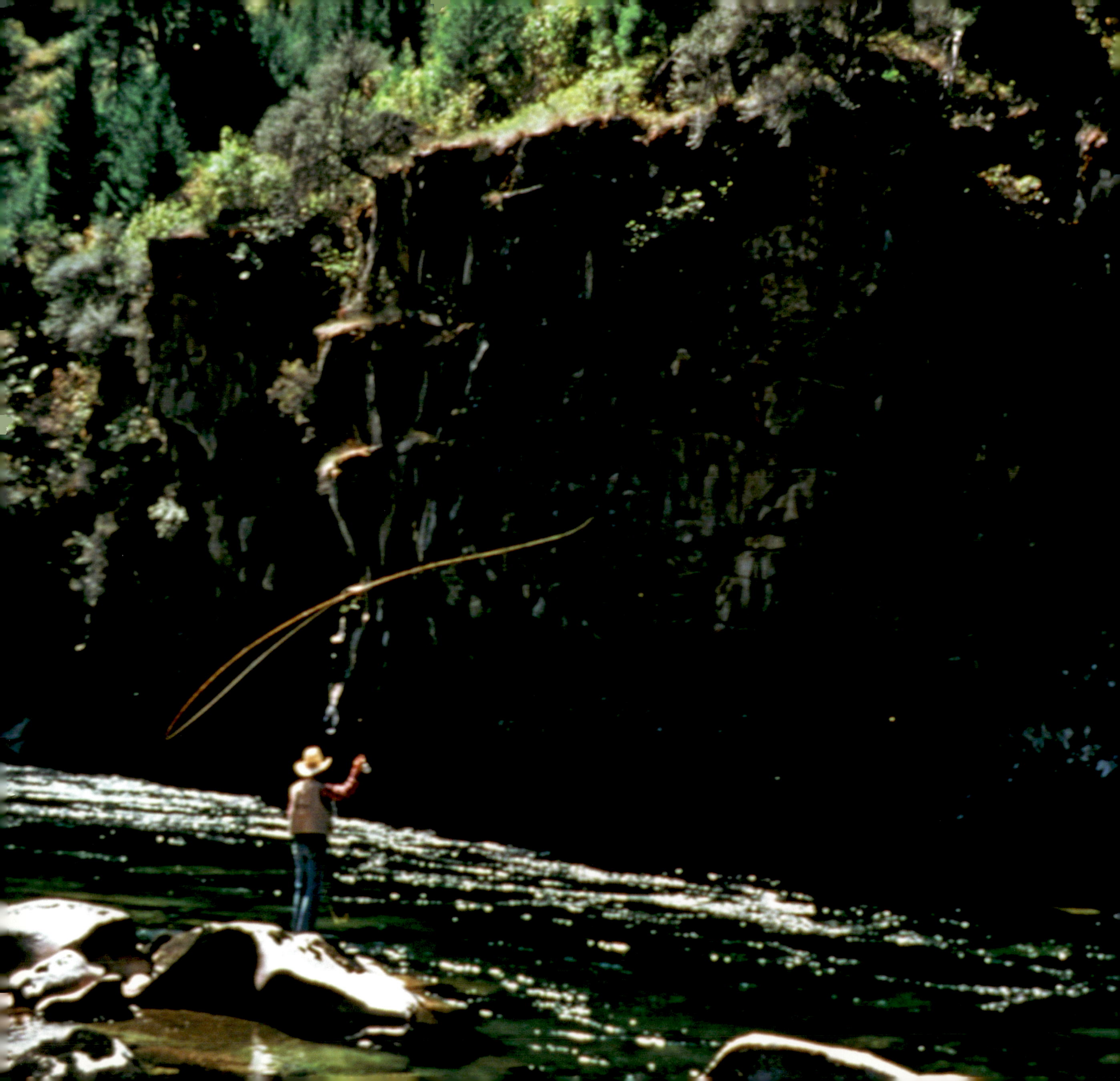

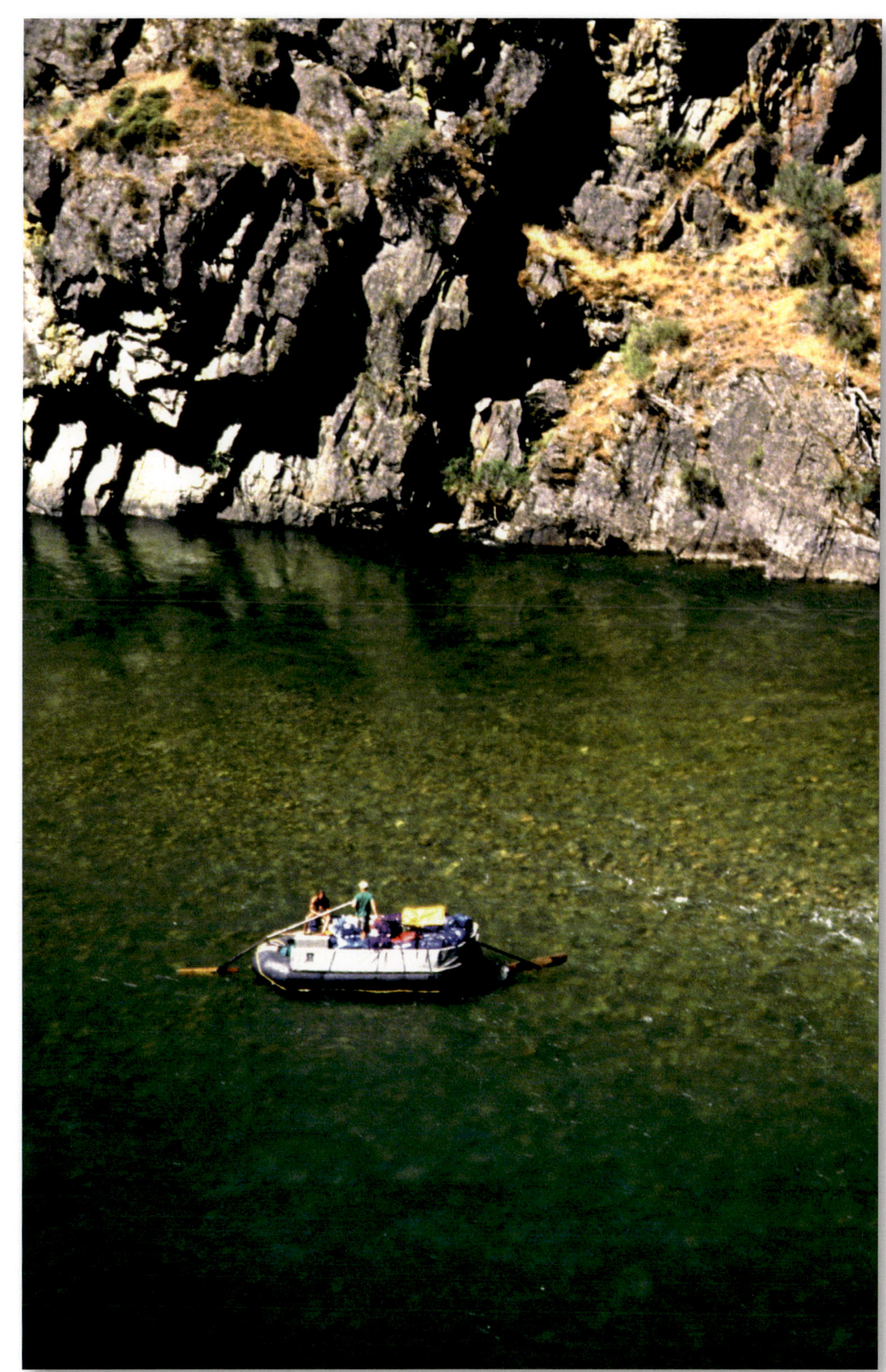

LEFT: A fisherman casts into a deep pool, hoping to pull out a cutthroat trout or two

RIGHT: Sweep Boat floating over a shallow stretch

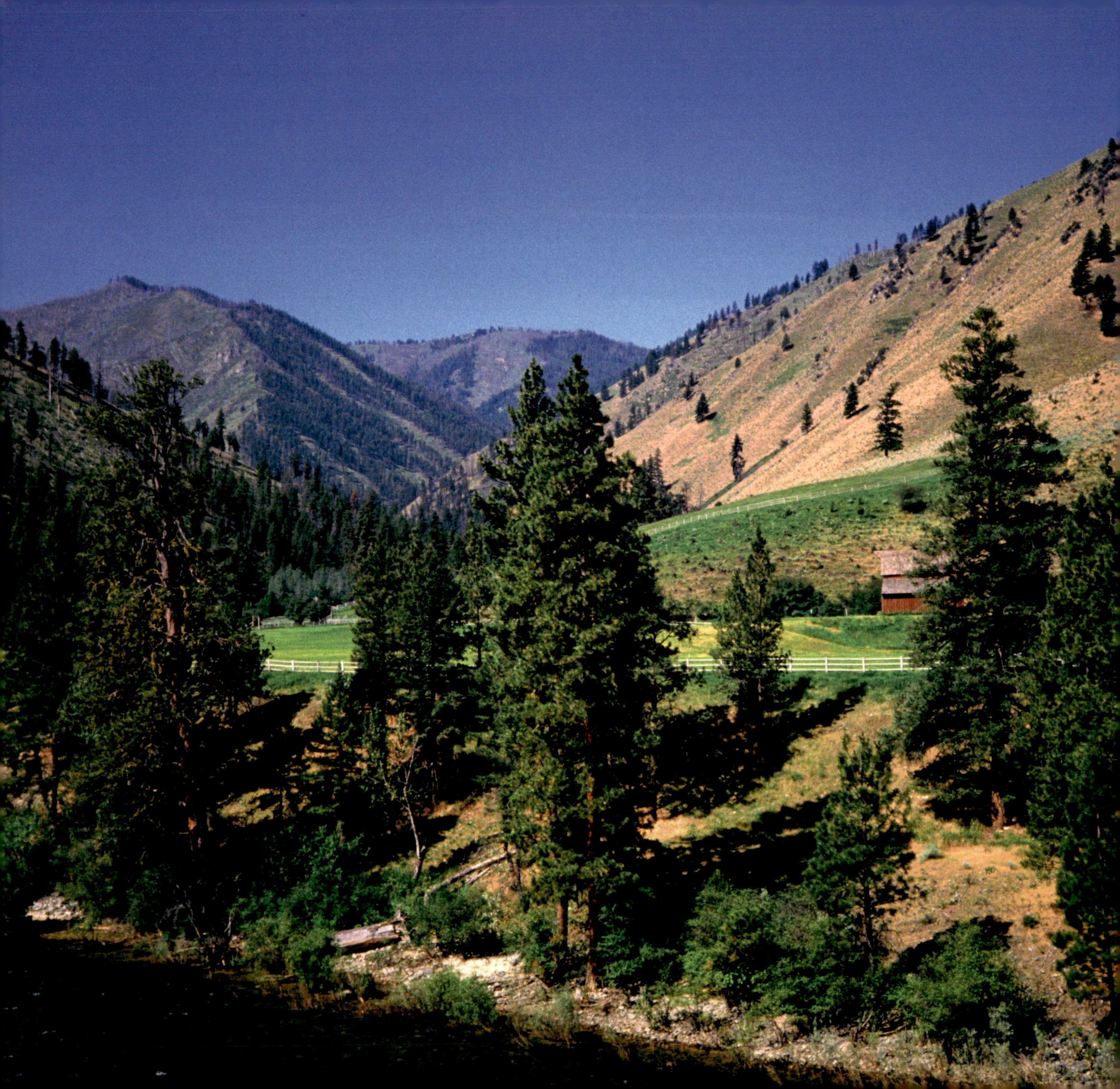

LEFT: Middle Fork Ranch (mile 33)

RIGHT: Author's daughter, Erin, bridge jumping (White Creek Pack Bridge, mile 47)

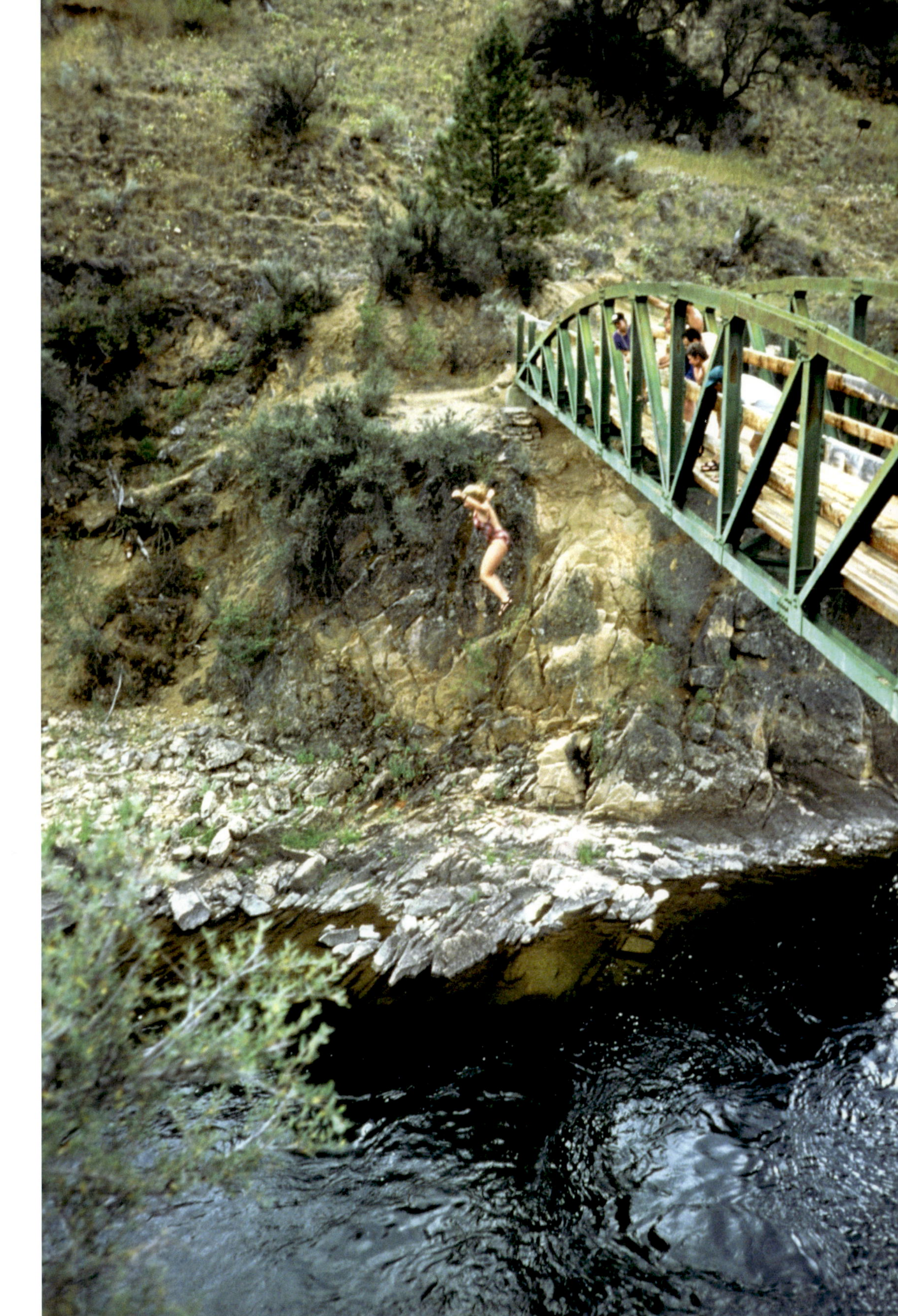

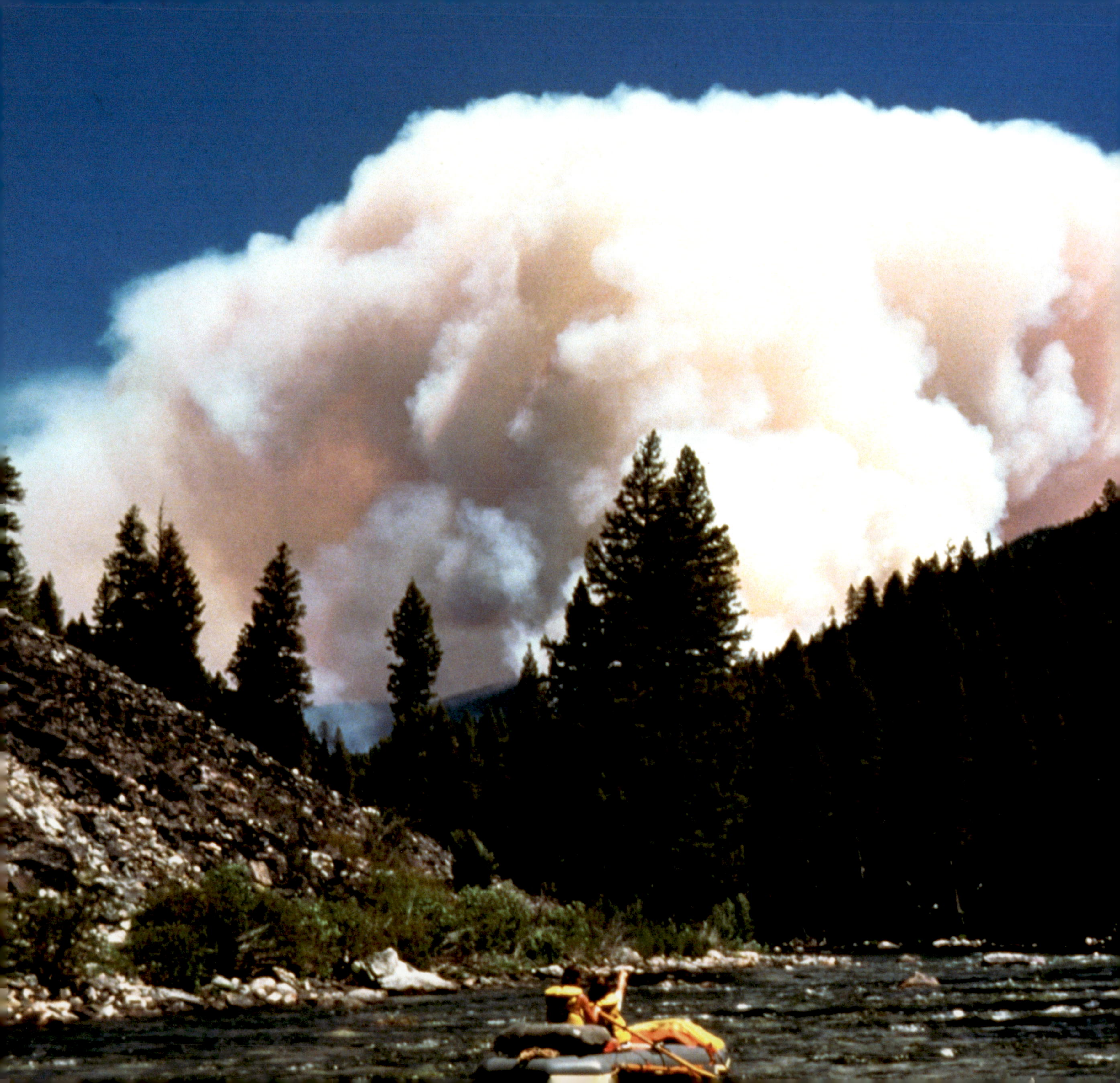

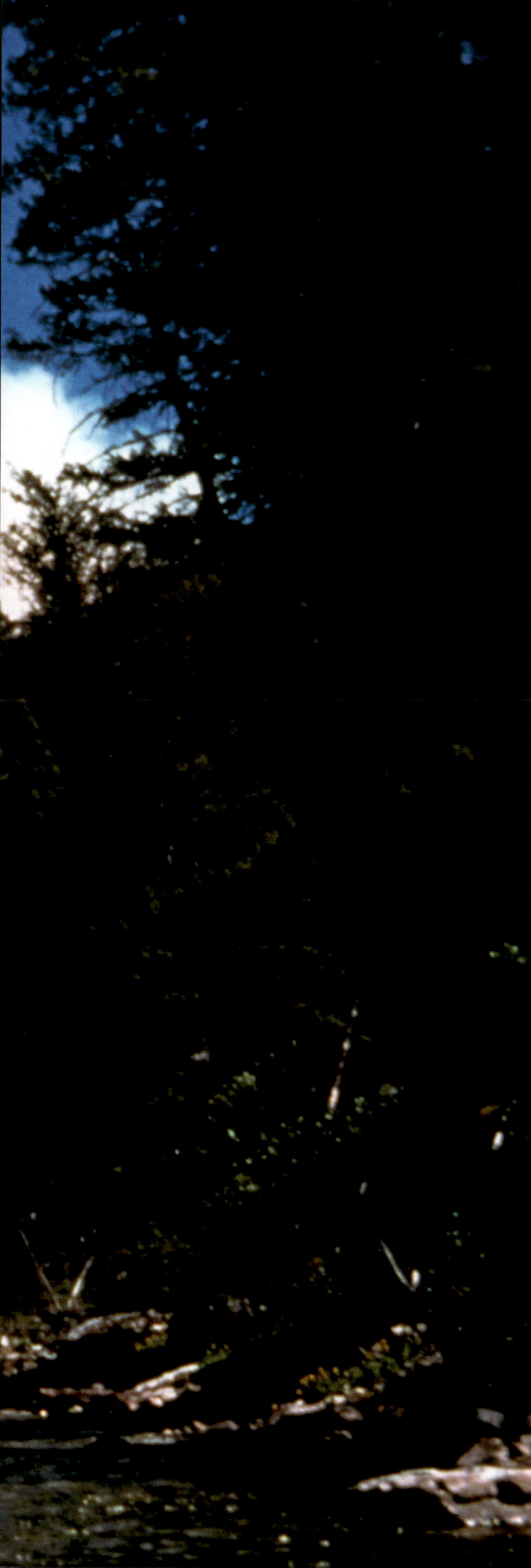

Mortar Creek Forest Fire, July 1979

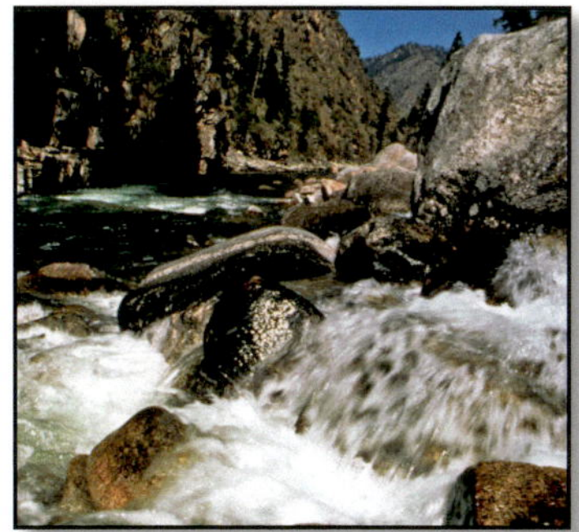

The Middle Fork canyon plunges 3,000 feet over its 100 miles, cutting a narrow swath through granite called the Idaho Batholith, the largest granite deposit in the nation. This formation has been severely eroded, exposing underlying rock formations laid down by four ages, the Precambrian, Permian, Triassic and Cretaceous periods. Some regard the Idaho Batholith as a sheet of granite several thousand feet thick, an intrusion of magma that rose to the Earth's crust where it found native rocks with the same density as the magma, and then spread horizontally.

The canyon itself is relatively young. Water and glaciers carved out the canyon cutting a deep and narrow slot suspected to begin flowing about 2.5 million years ago through a valley. Much of central Idaho, including the area around the Middle Fork, is richly upholstered in a thick mantel of soil and deeply weathered rock.

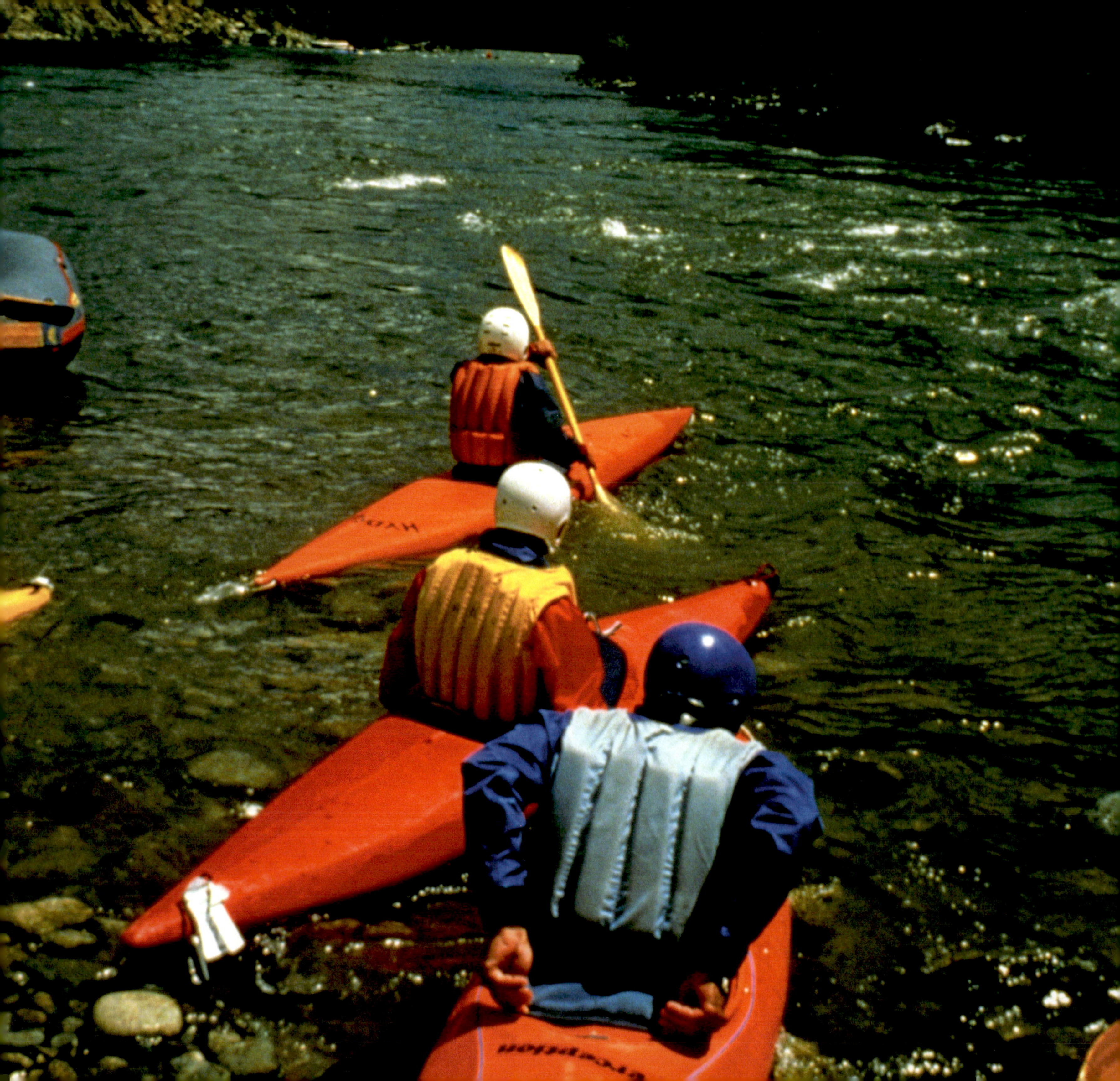

LEFT: Kayakers make their way through the Middle Canyon.

BELOW: Author's wife, Jodie, making her way down-stream in a Rubber Ducky

RIGHT: Catch and Release– Native Cutthroat

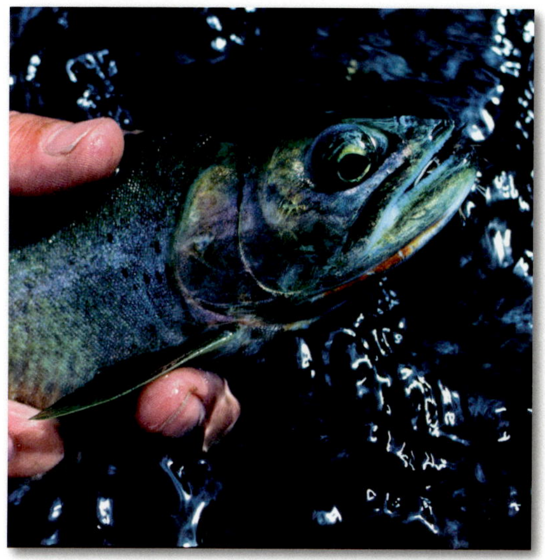

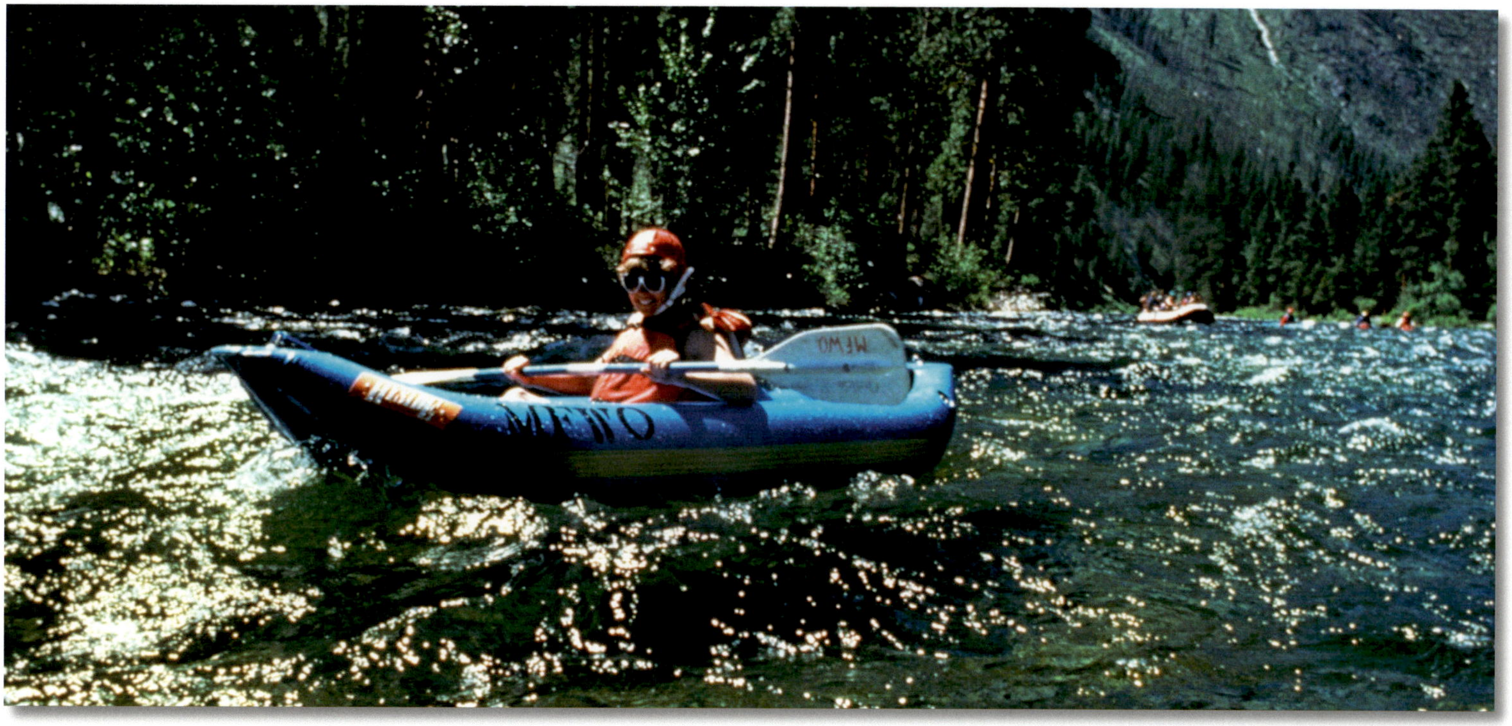

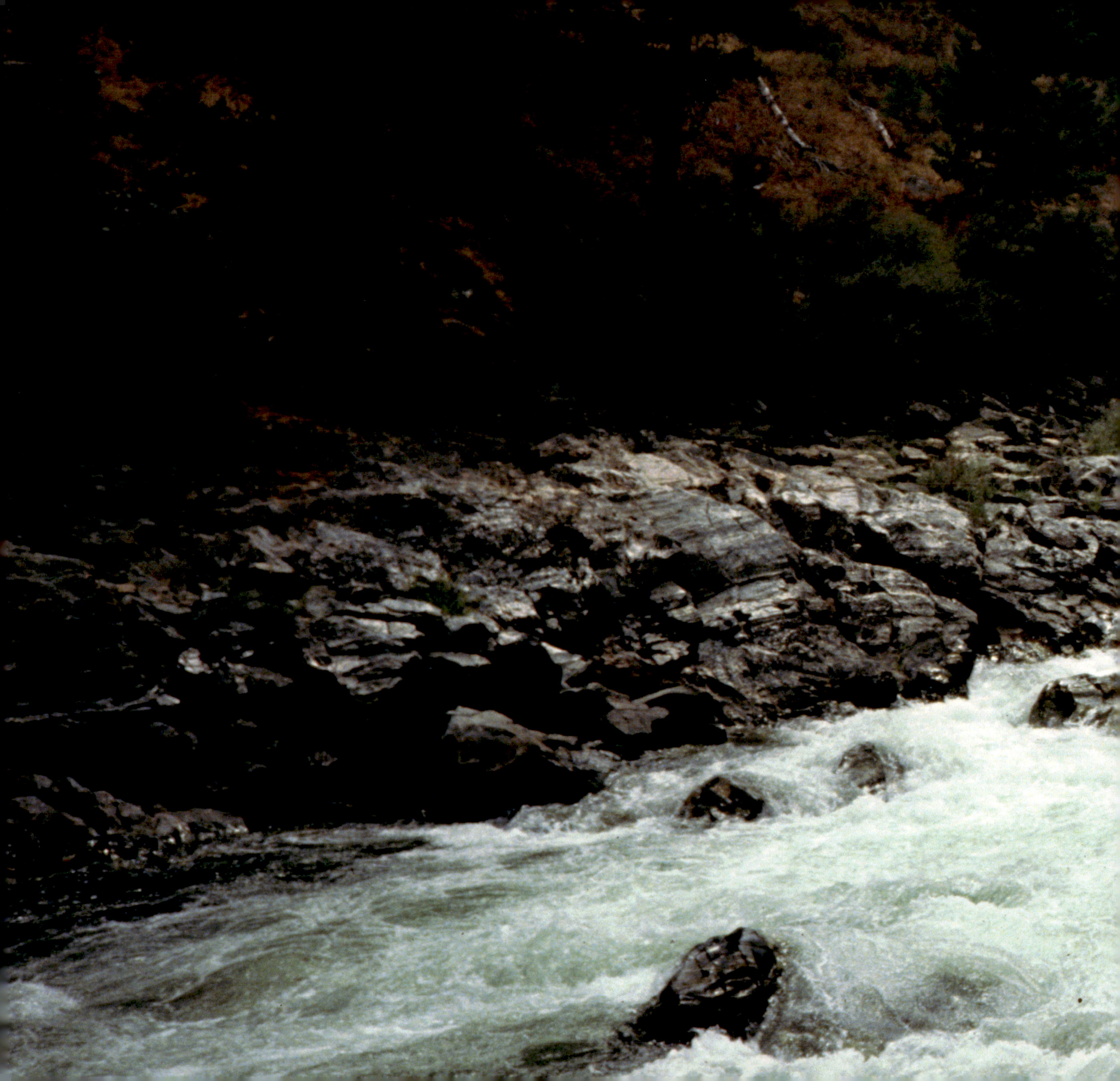

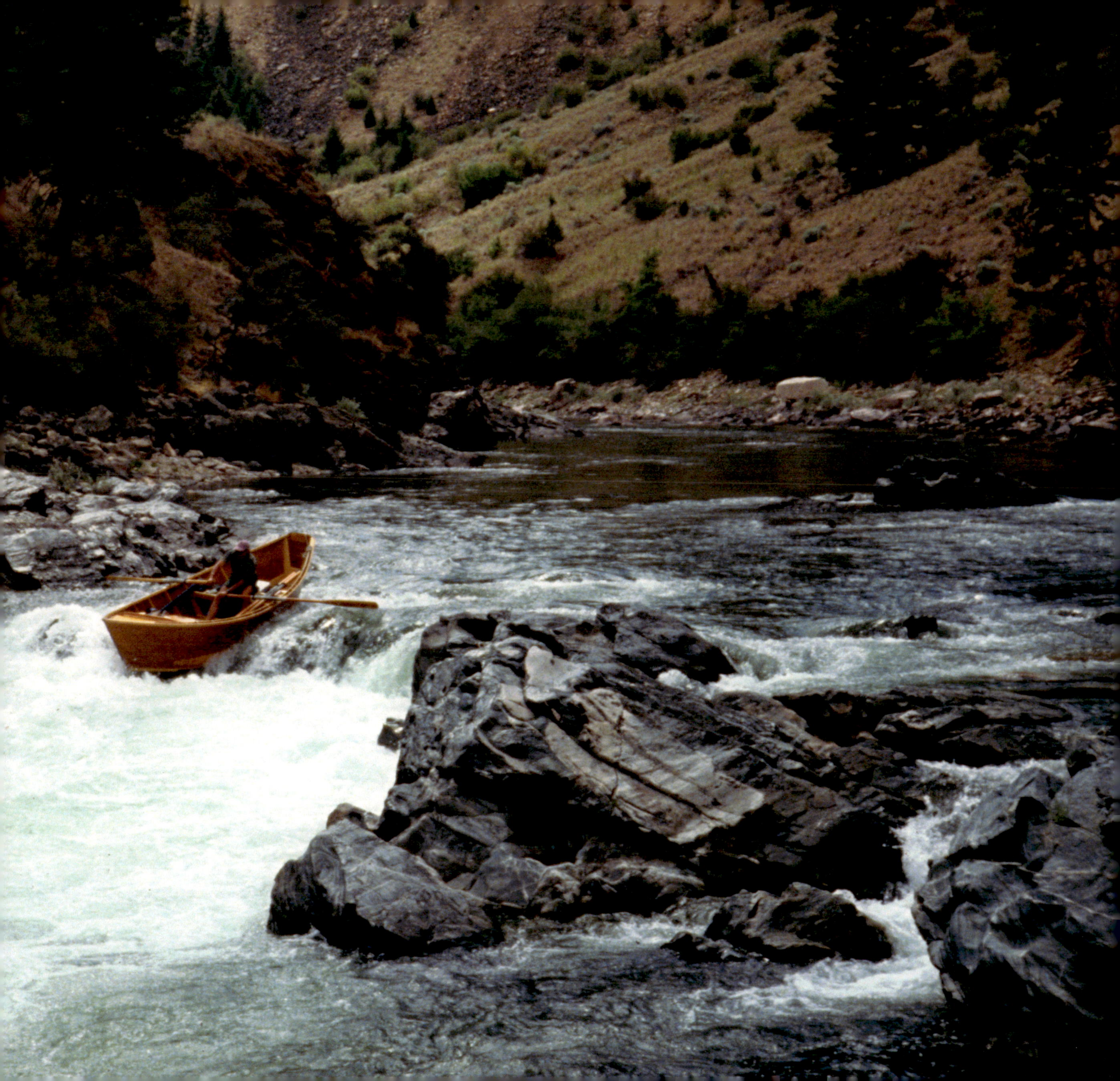

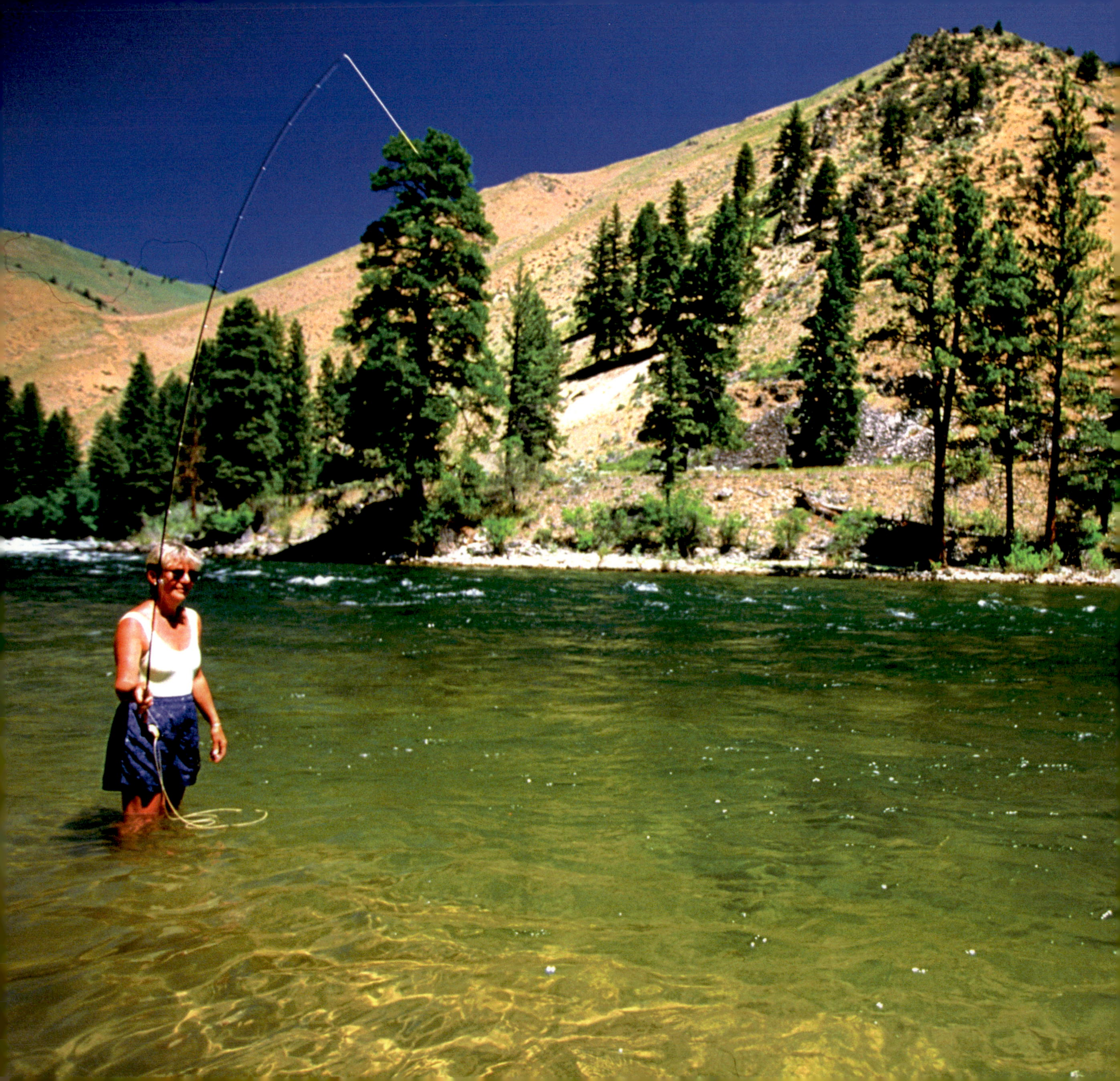

LEFT: Liz Robbins landing a cutthroat

BELOW: Royal Robbins

RIGHT: Tamara Robbins admiring one of the many geological wonders

PREVIOUS SPREAD: Outfitter Kurt Selish navigating Tappen Falls (mile 58)

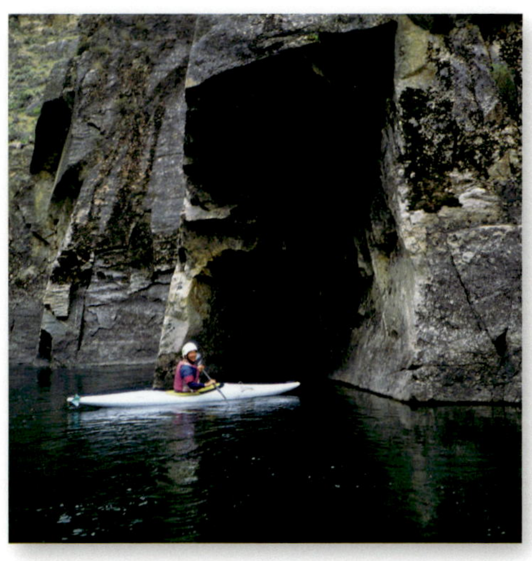

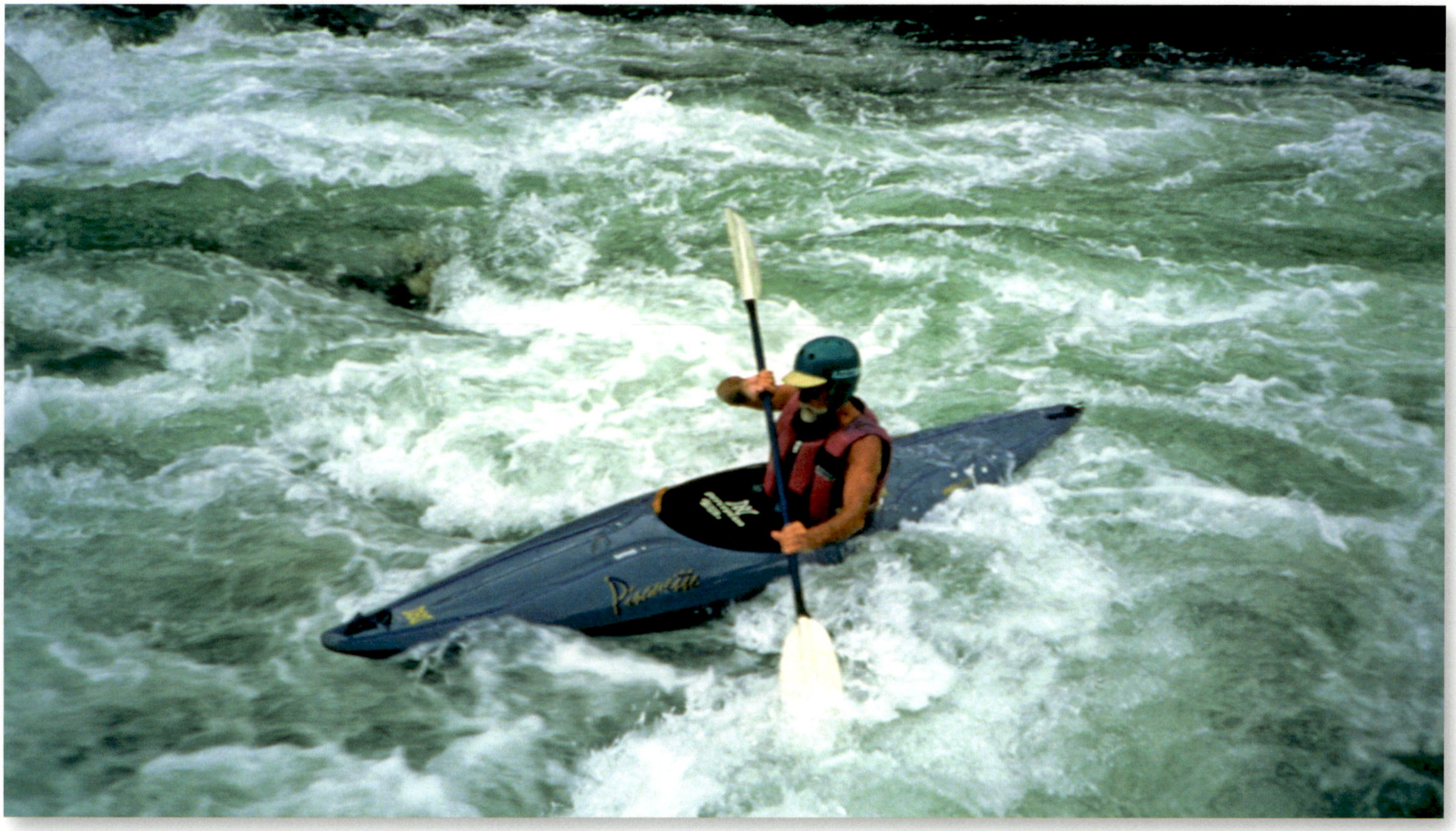

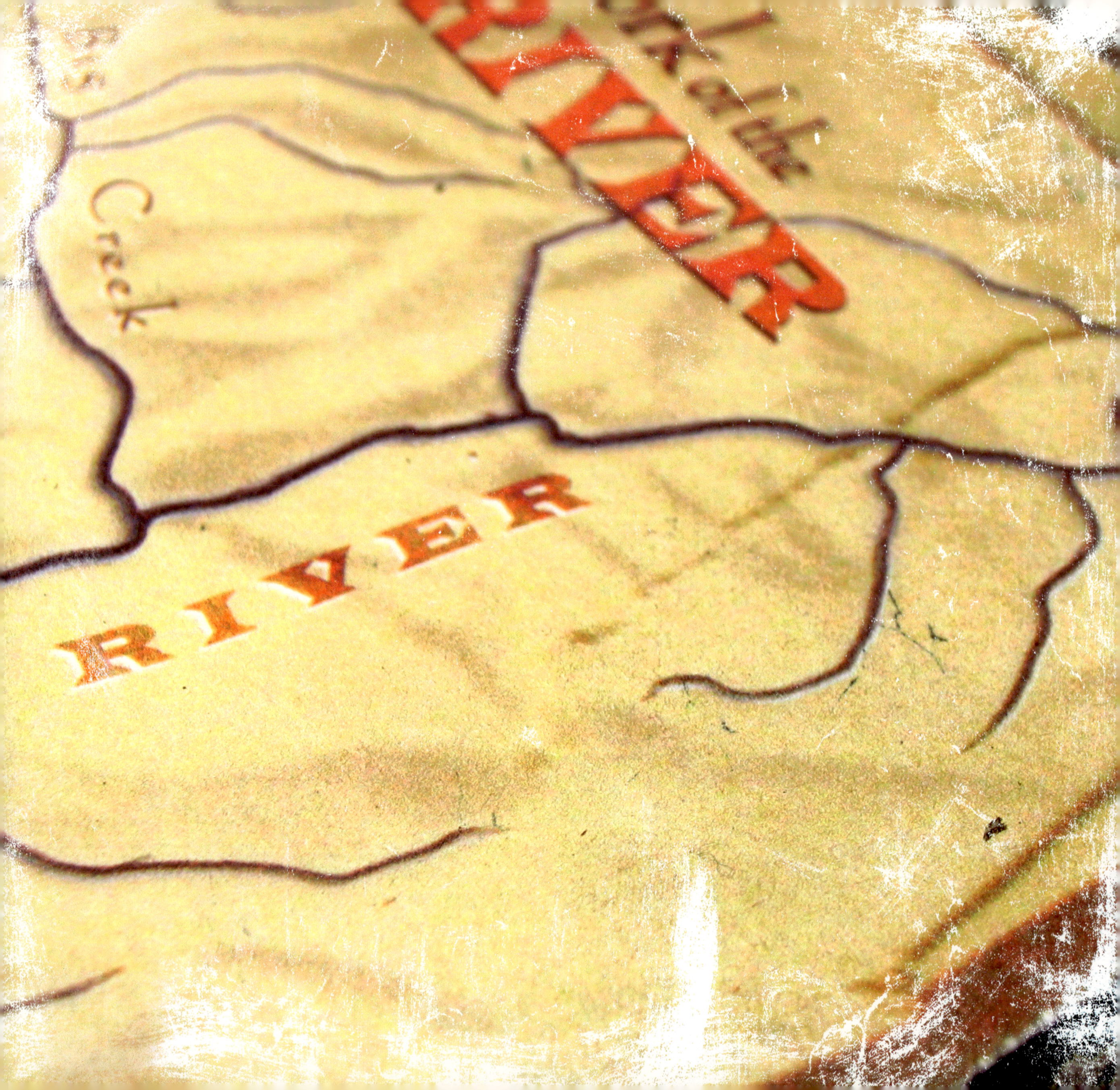
RIVER
Creek
RIVER

THE LOWER CANYON

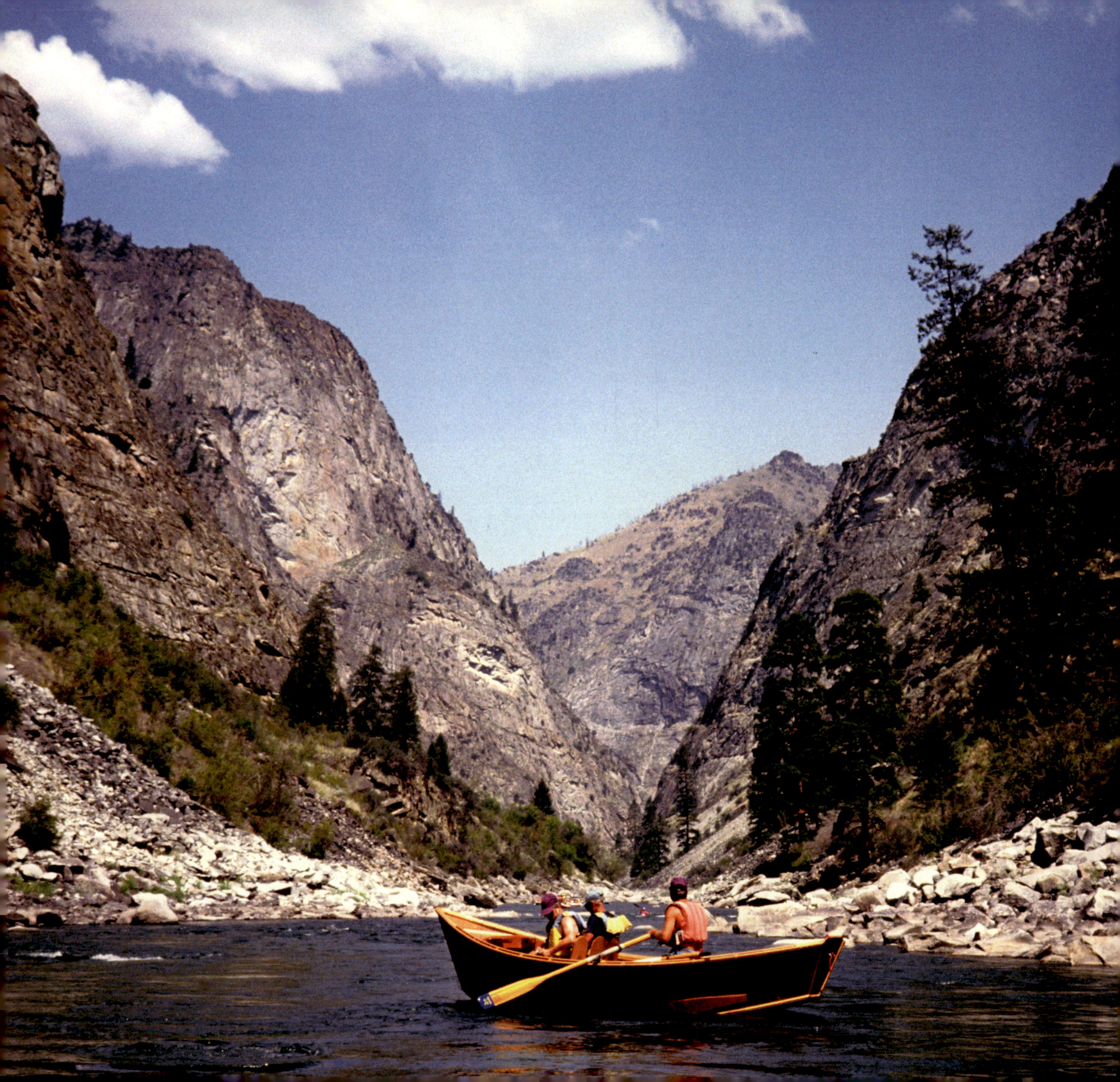

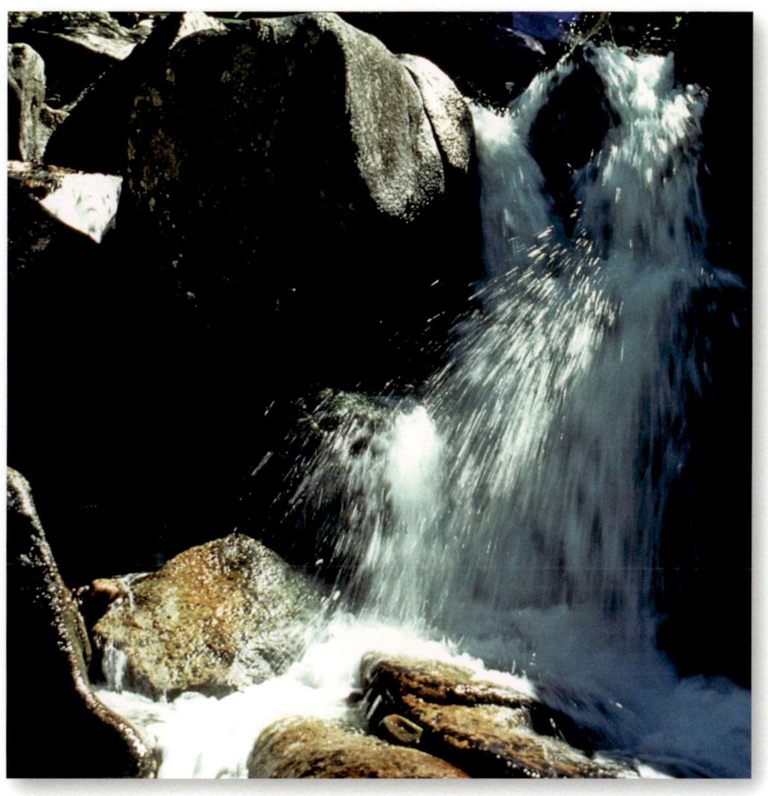

..The Lower Canyon (mile 68–100) includes the infamous Impassable Canyon begining at mile 78.

The lower canyon (mile 68–96) begins at Haystack Rapids just below the Flying B Ranch. Haystack Rapids is a long rock garden requiring significant maneuvering. In recent years, Pole Creek, which feeds into Haystack Rapids, has blown-out, changing Haystack from year to year. Rattlesnake Cave is located on the right bank (mile 74) containing numerous Indian pictographs yet to be interpreted. Directly after Waterfall Rapids (mile 77), Waterfall Creek tumbles 300 feet to meet the passing river. The gateway to the Impassable Canyon begins directly below Big Creek (mile 78) and runs to the mouth (mile 96). The Impassable Canyon holds a number of large river boulders producing 13 major rapids including Haystack, Jack Creek, Waterfall Creek, Porcupine, Redside, Weber, Upper Cliffside, Lower Cliffside, Rubber, Hancock, Devil's Tooth, House Rocks and Jump-Off.

At the end of the canyon, the mouth of the crystalline Middle Fork enters the more opaque Main Salmon, the River of No Return. Boaters must float four miles of the Main Salmon in order to take out at Cache Bar thus completing the 100-mile, five-night and six-day trip.

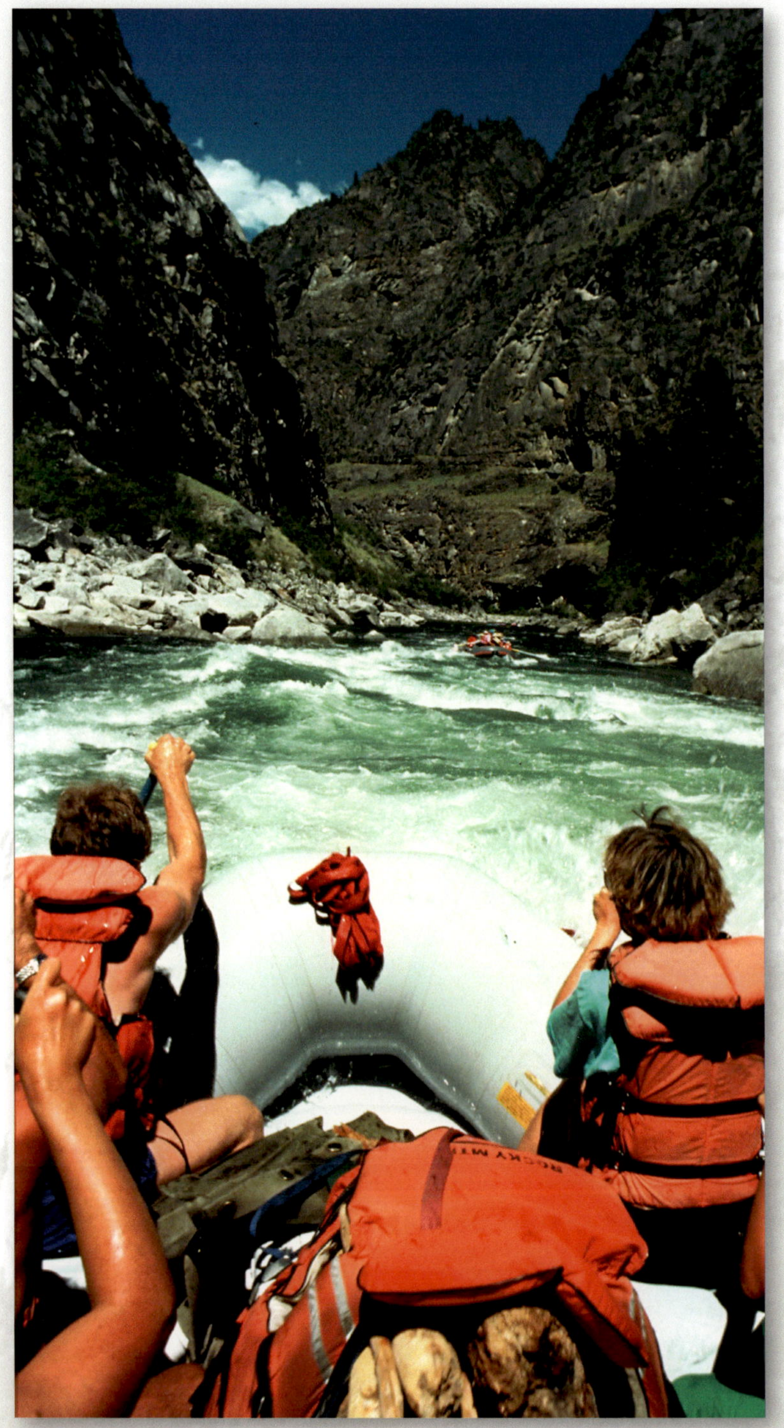

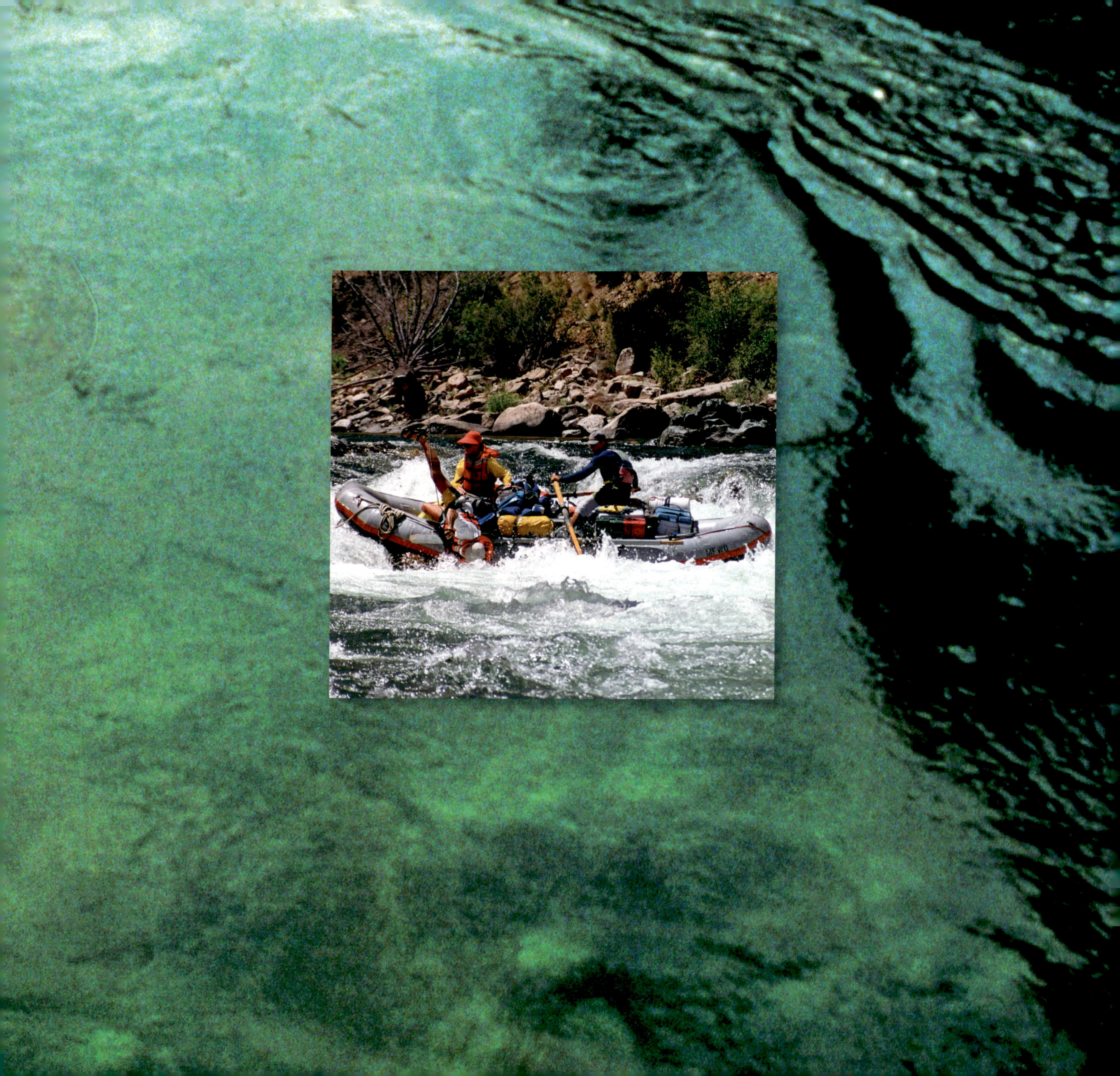

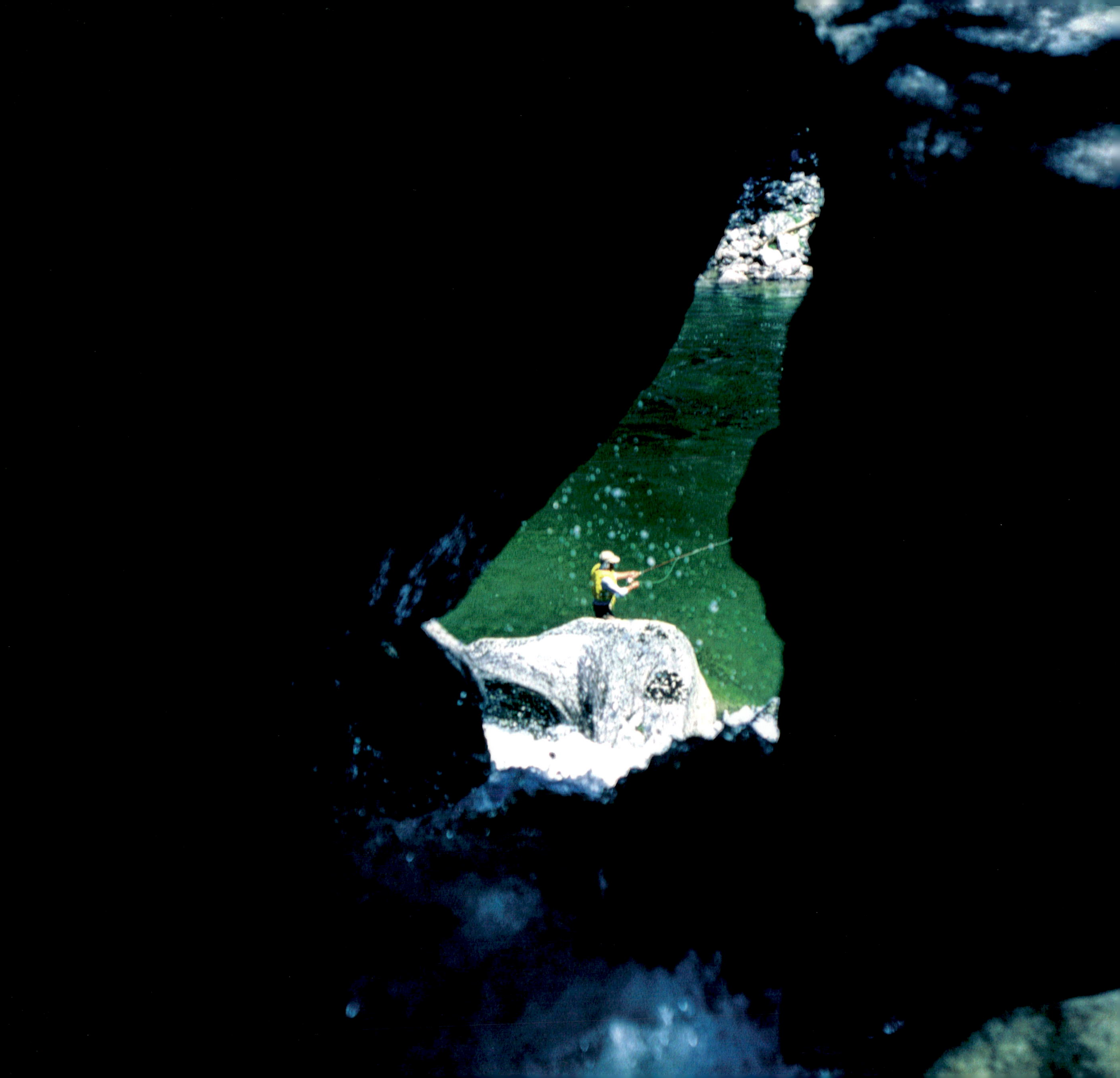

LEFT: Fly-fisherman's Heaven

RIGHT: Upper Cliffside Rapids (mile 88)

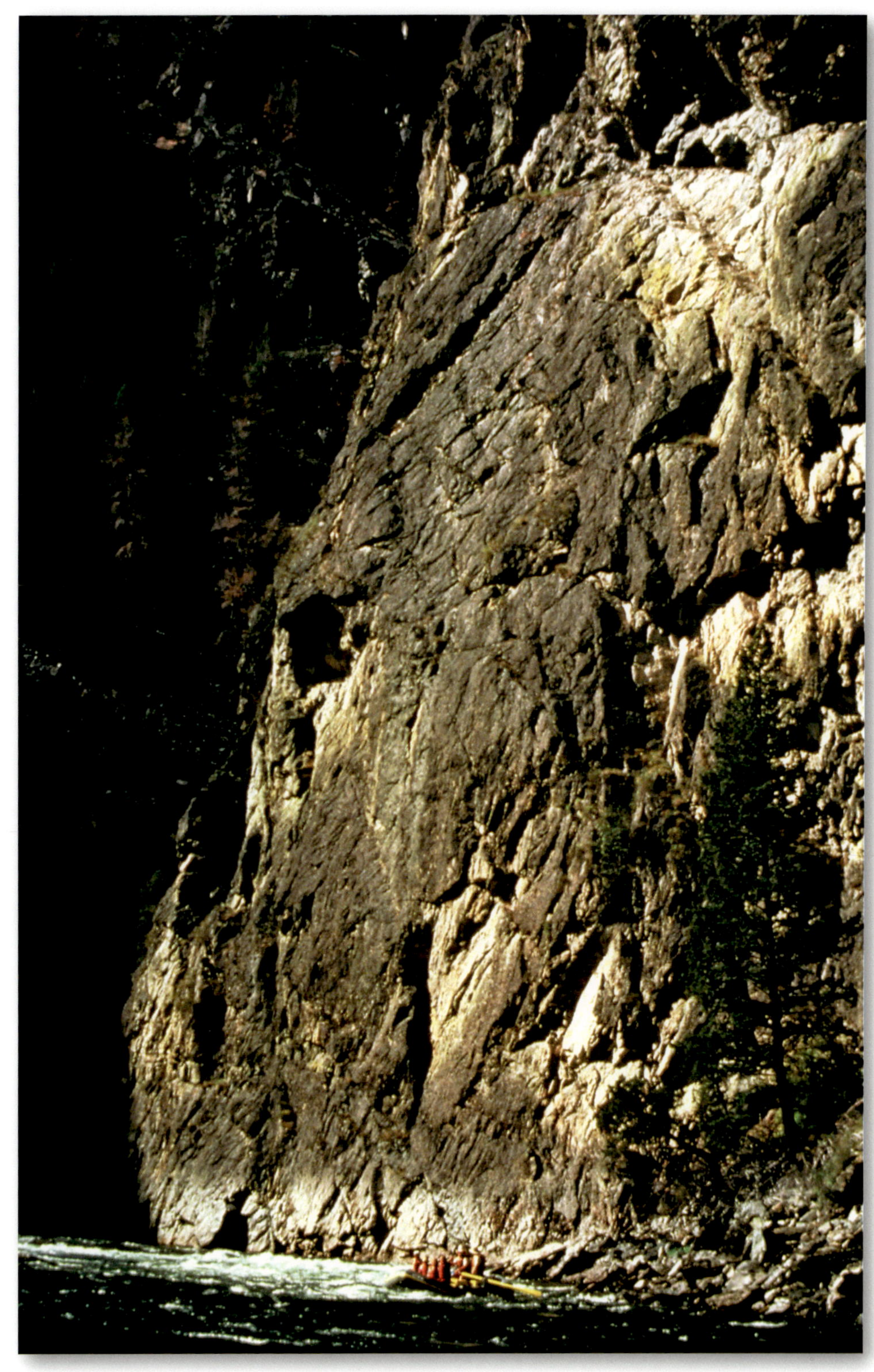

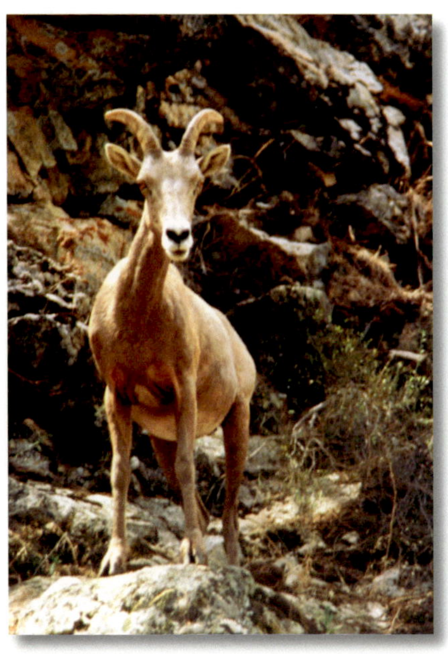

LEFT: Mountain Goats frequent the rugged lower-canyon country

BELOW: Splashin' through Jump-Off rapid (mile 91)

RIGHT: The sun luminates the canyon walls before setting

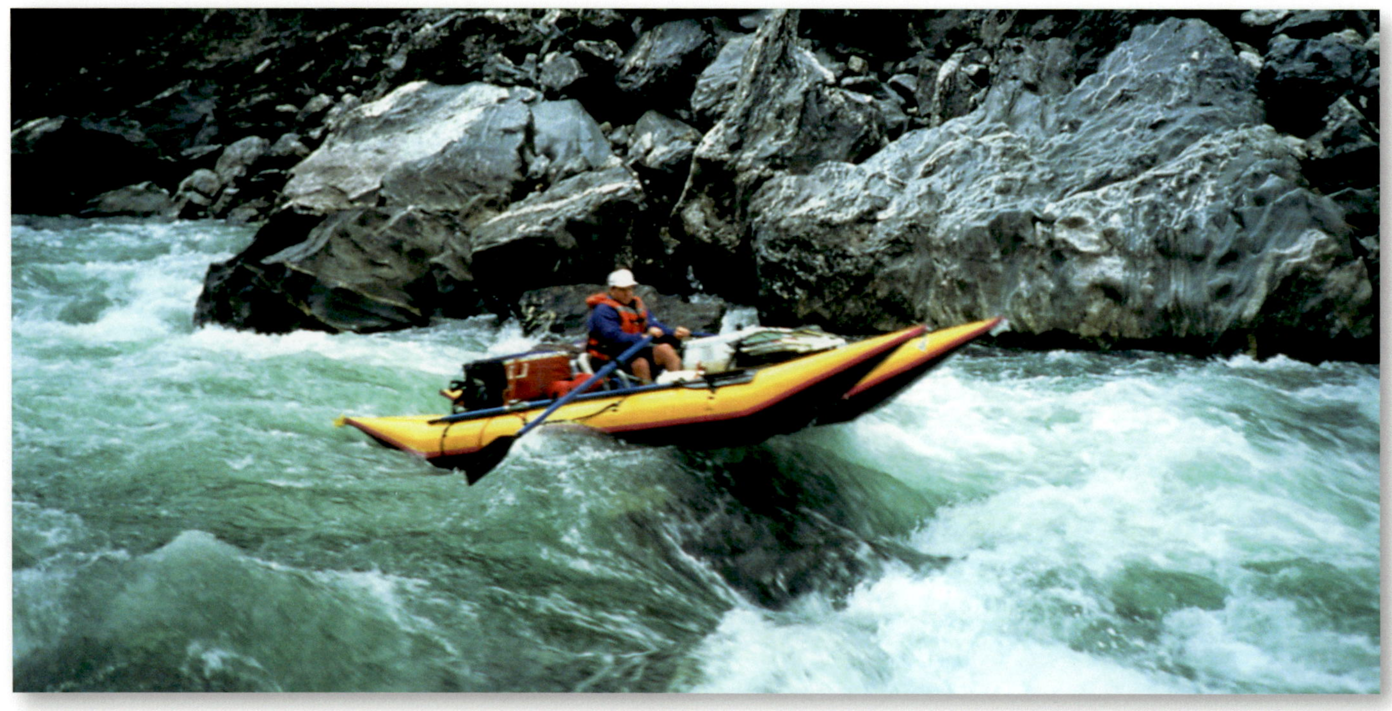

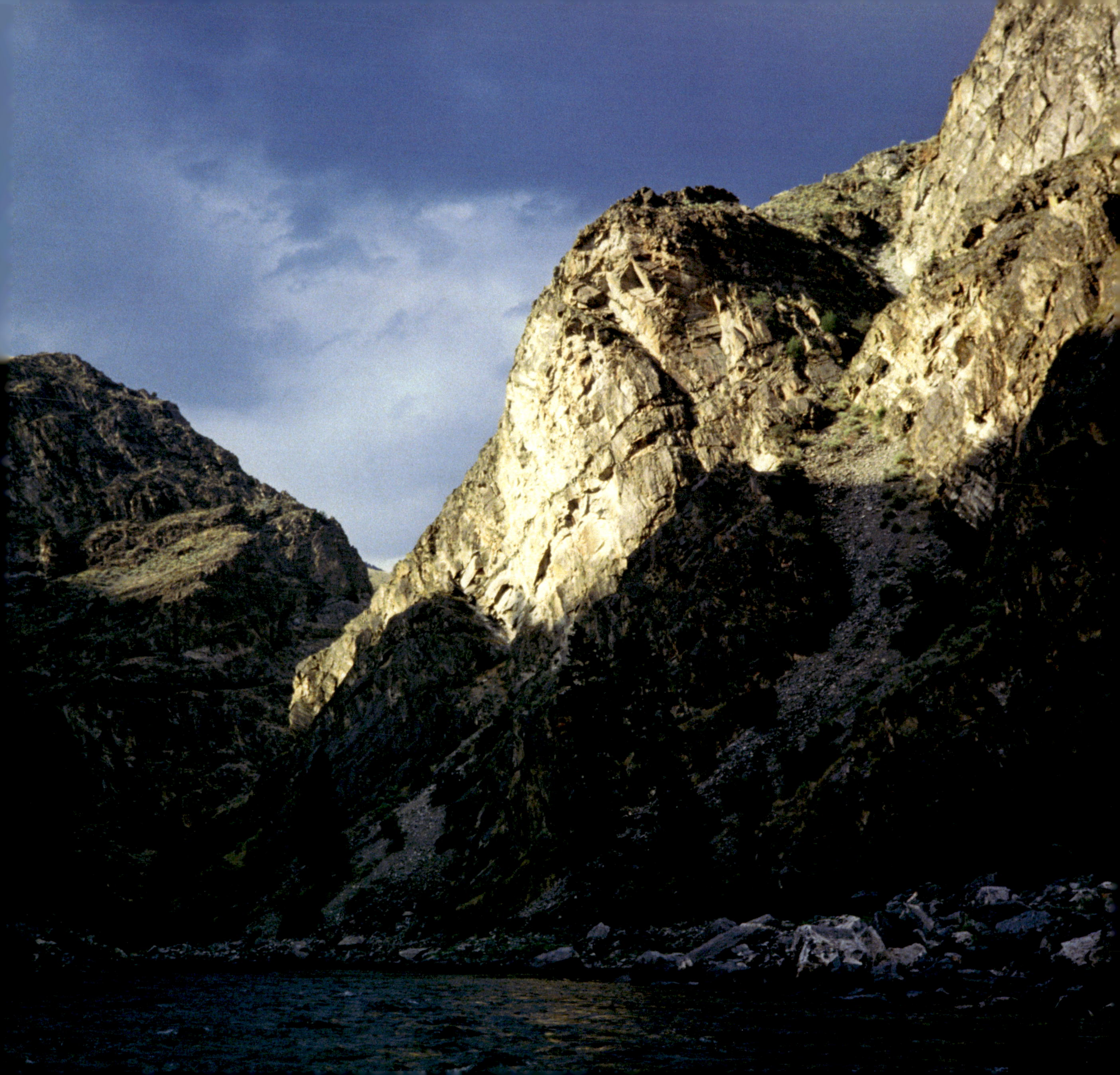

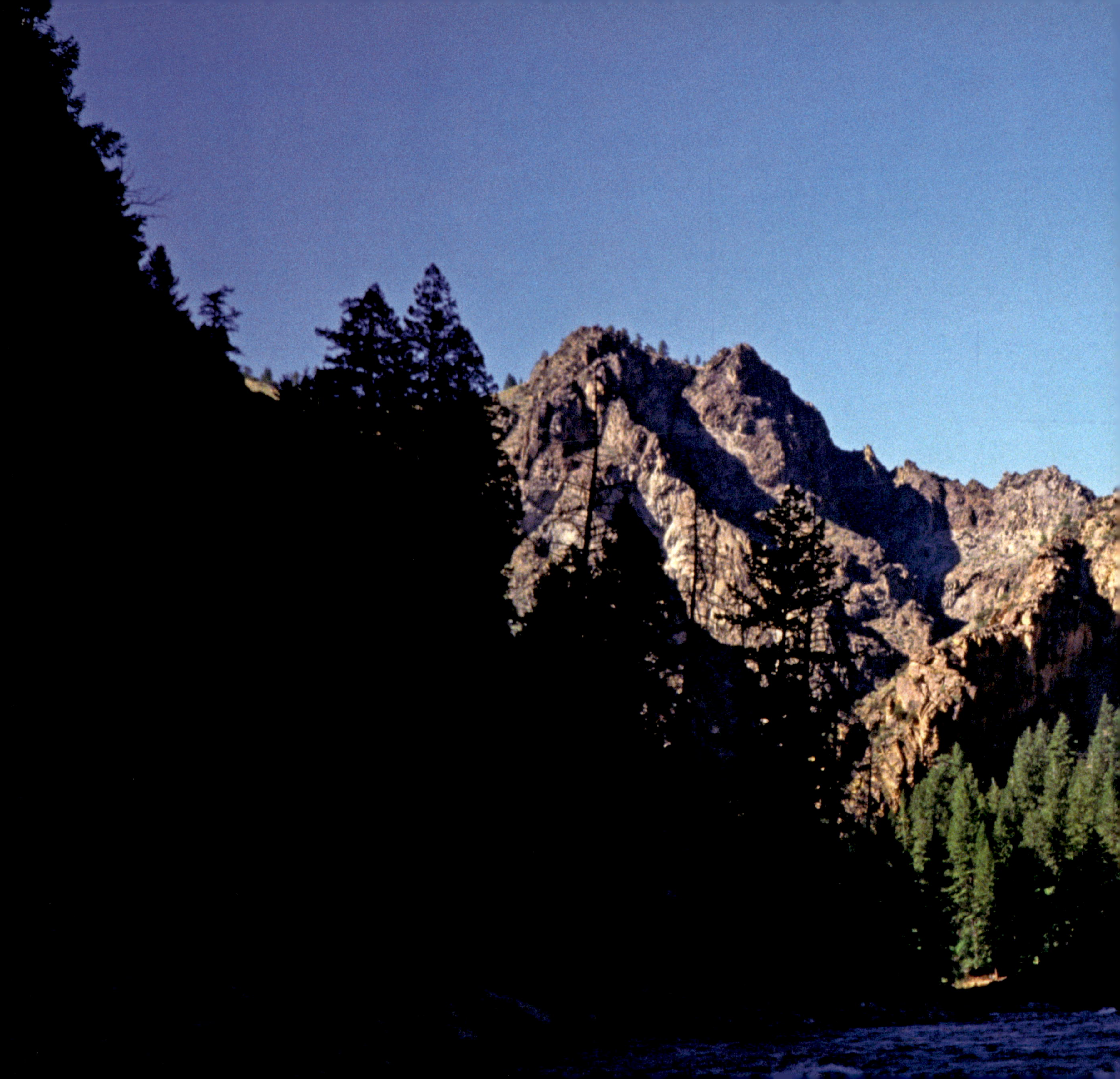

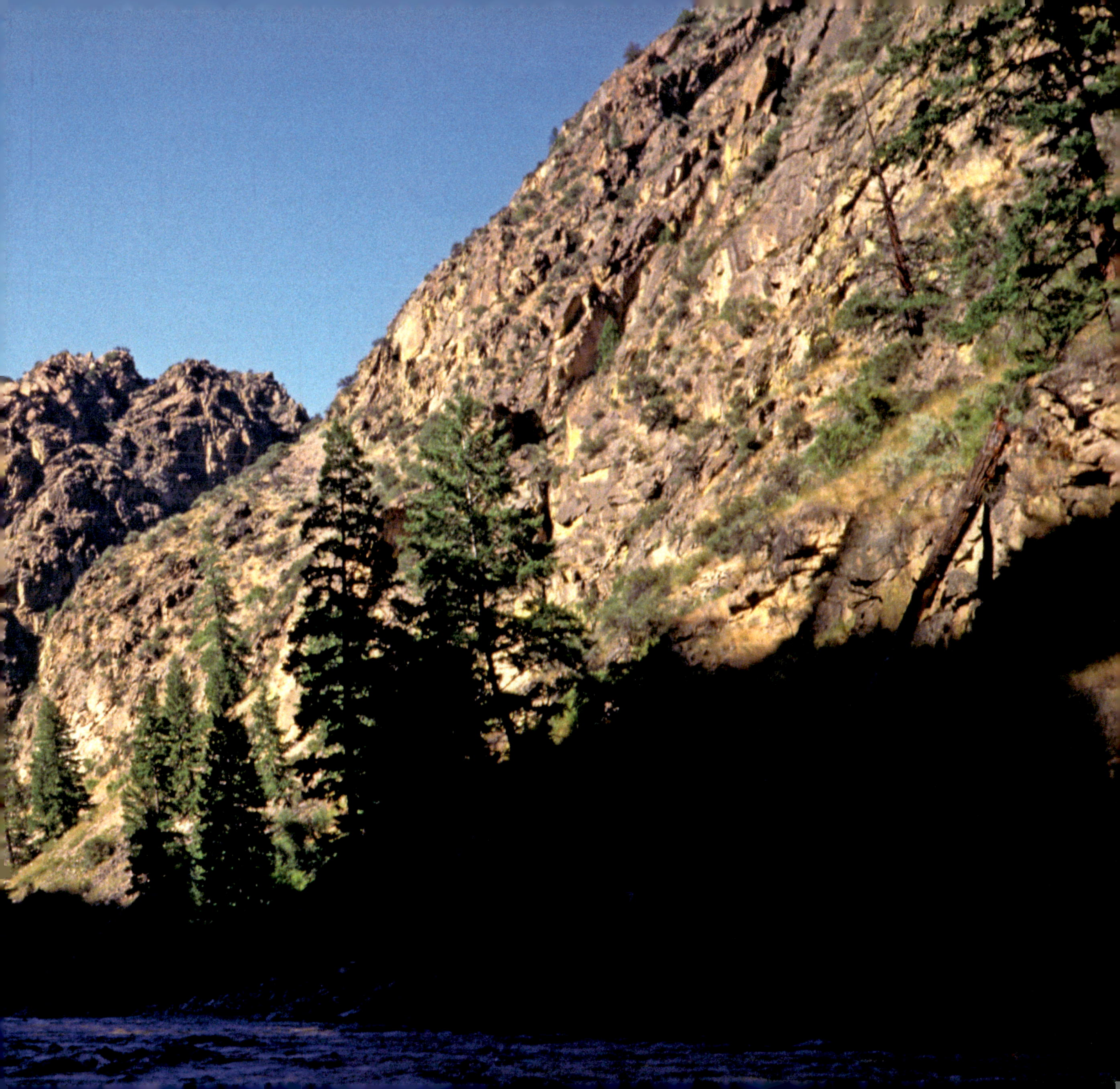

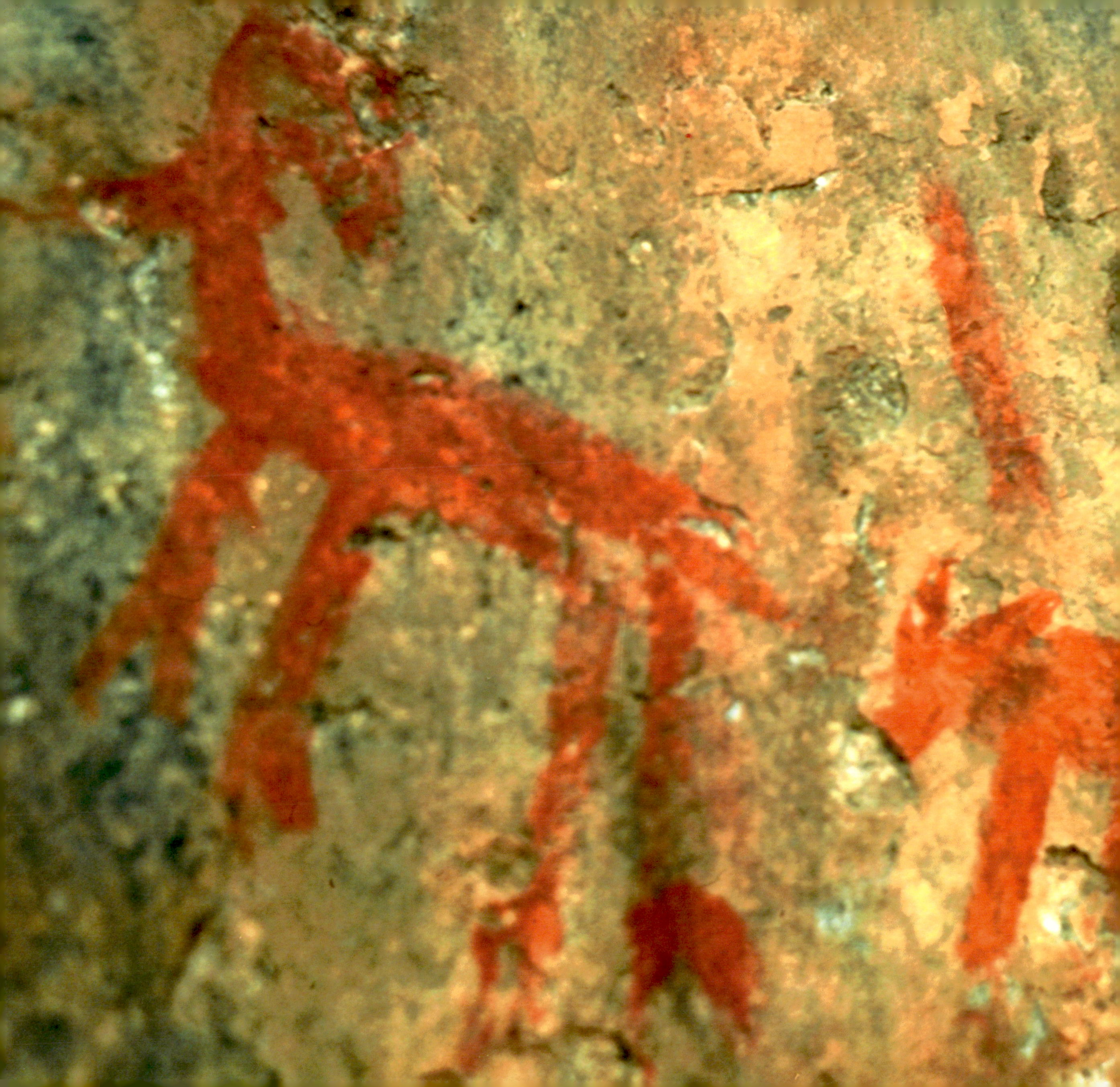

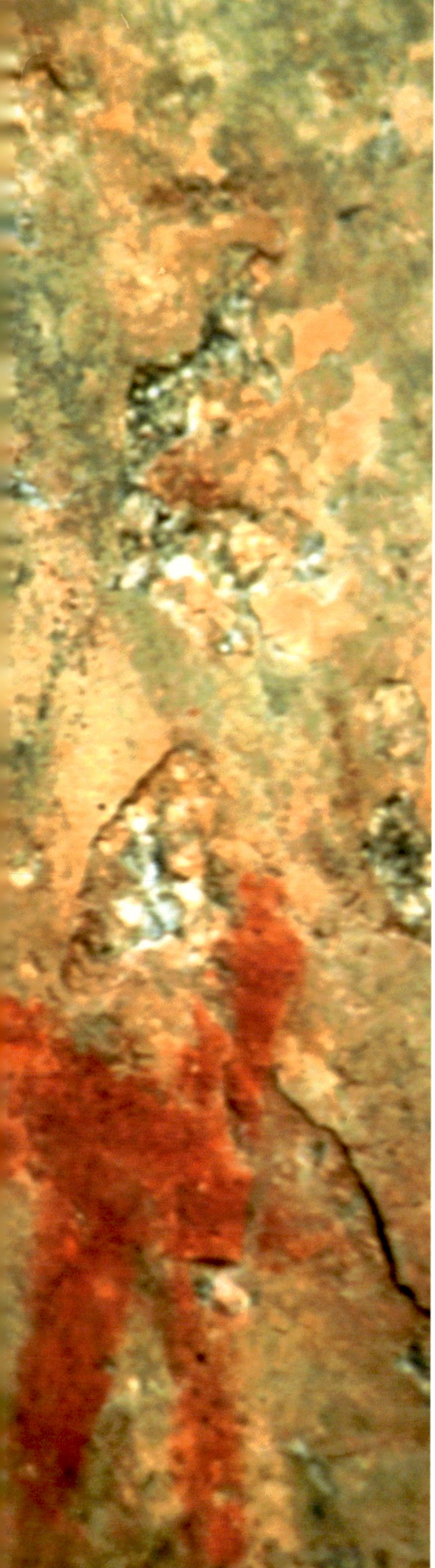

Inhabiting the canyon for thousands of years, the Sheepeater Indians were named due to their skill in subsisting on the Big Horn Sheep. Their name, in the Shoshone language, was Tuku-deka, literally meaning sheepeater. Living in caves along the river and hunting along streambeds, the Sheepeater Indians were the last native resistance in Idaho. Due to their isolated existence in the rugged canyon, they developed their own dialect and customs until displaced in the 1879.

A massacre of five Chinese miners on Loon Creek on February 12, 1879 prompted an army unit out in the spring to pursue the Sheepeaters. Deep snow held back the search particularly since they lived in rough country largely unknown to the whites. Being just months after the intense and long Nez Perce War, led by Chief Joseph, the Sheepeaters decided to resist. A dozen ambushed and defeated forty-eight mounted infantry who were accompanied by twenty scouts and packers.

After this engagement, one energetic Sheepeater on July 29, halted the army retreat on a mountain ridge. The resulting battle of Vinegar Hill turned into an incredible siege in which a handful of Indians pinned down the entire army for fourteen-hours without water. It forced them to drink their only liquid, a jug of vinegar, thus naming the hill.

The tracking and scouting continued on into the autumn months. The Indians had scattered, making a definitive attack – and routing – impossible. The army was able to recapture some hidden caches of food, found some horses wandering in the wilderness, proving they were out of their element.

On September 24, the scouts sent out one of the captured women to locate her people. She was forced to leave her baby with the scouts to ensure her return. She came back that evening, with nothing to say.

It all ended the next day, anti-climatically. The scouts heard a whoop, which turned out to be made by a man named War Jack. War Jack told the scouts that he was tired of running and fighting. The Army Captain demanded an unconditional surrender. The Indians agreed, and the band of 51 Sheepeater tribal people, mostly women and children, left the Middle Fork country as captives of the U.S. Army.

Years later, local residents of the area admitted that whites looking to steal gold had killed the Chinese. The numerous pictographs found in the canyon have yet to be interpreted.

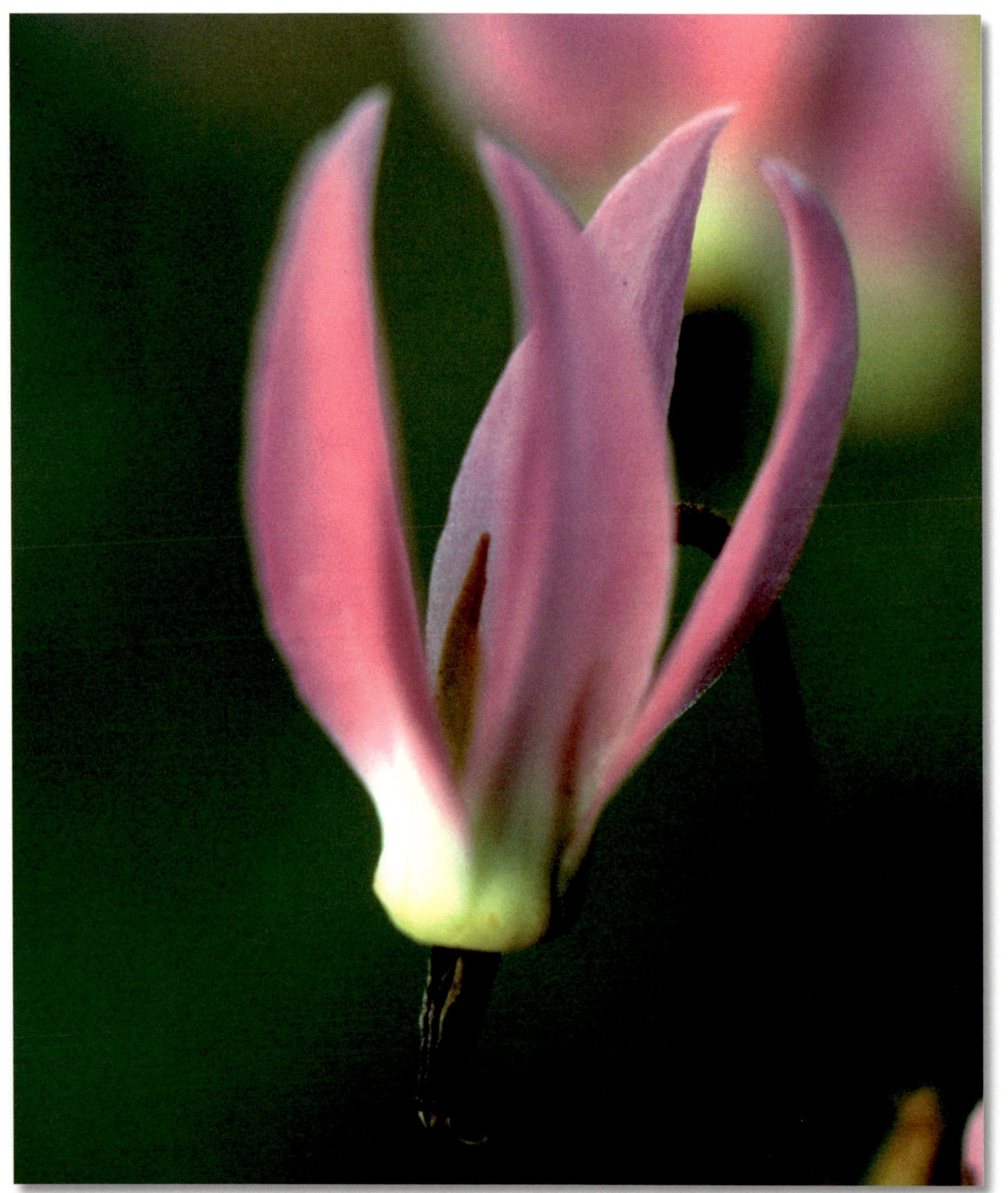

LEFT: Shooting Star

RIGHT: Very few experience the river in a classic wooden drift boat

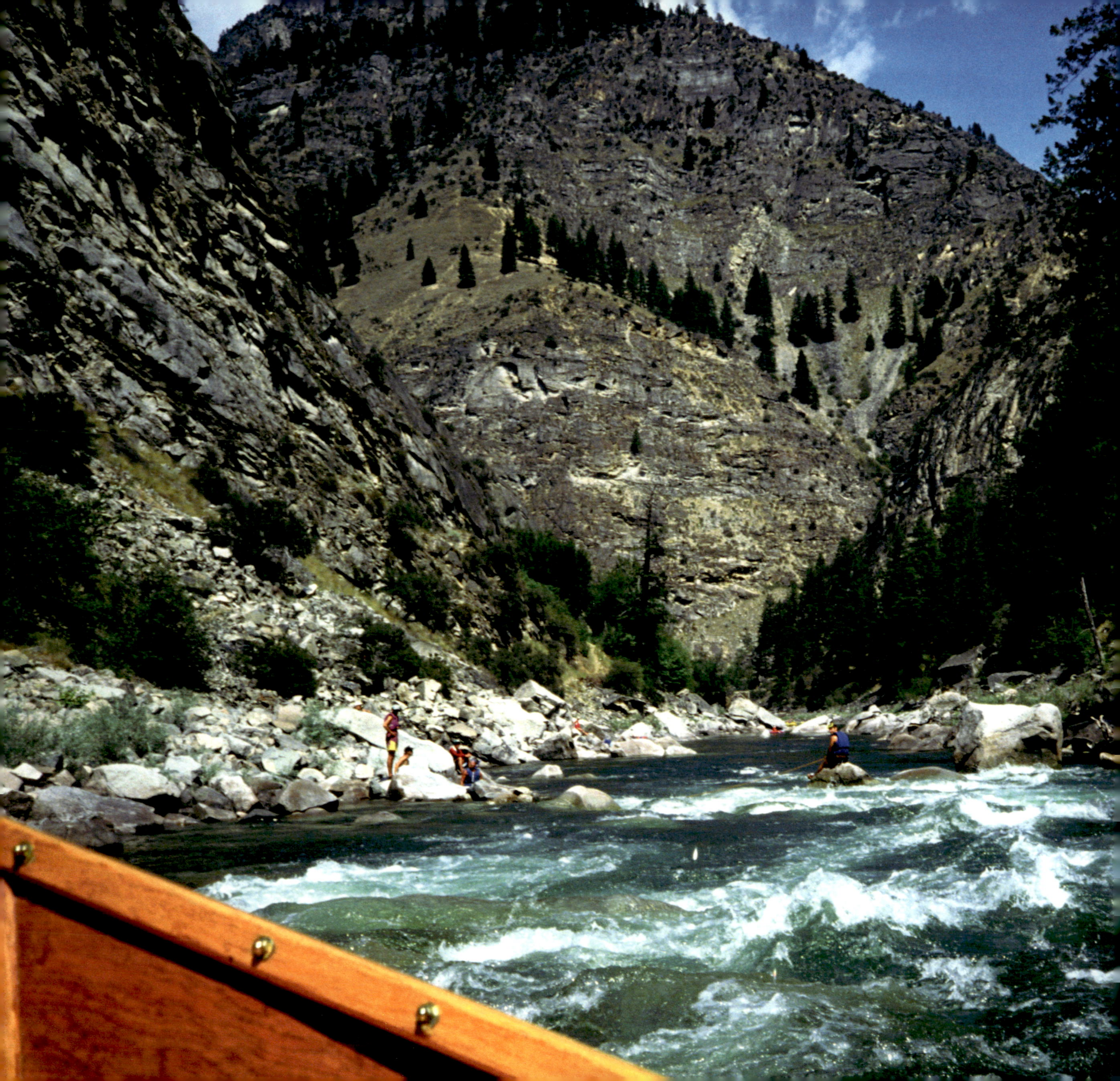

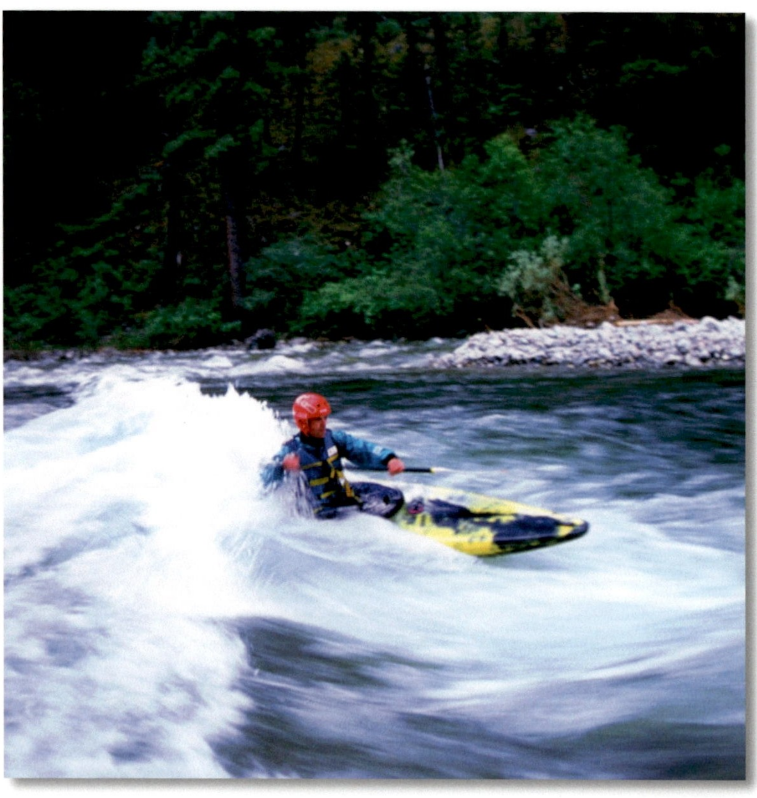

LEFT: A kayaker front surfs a standing wave

RIGHT: The river carving its way through the steep walls of the Impassable Canyon

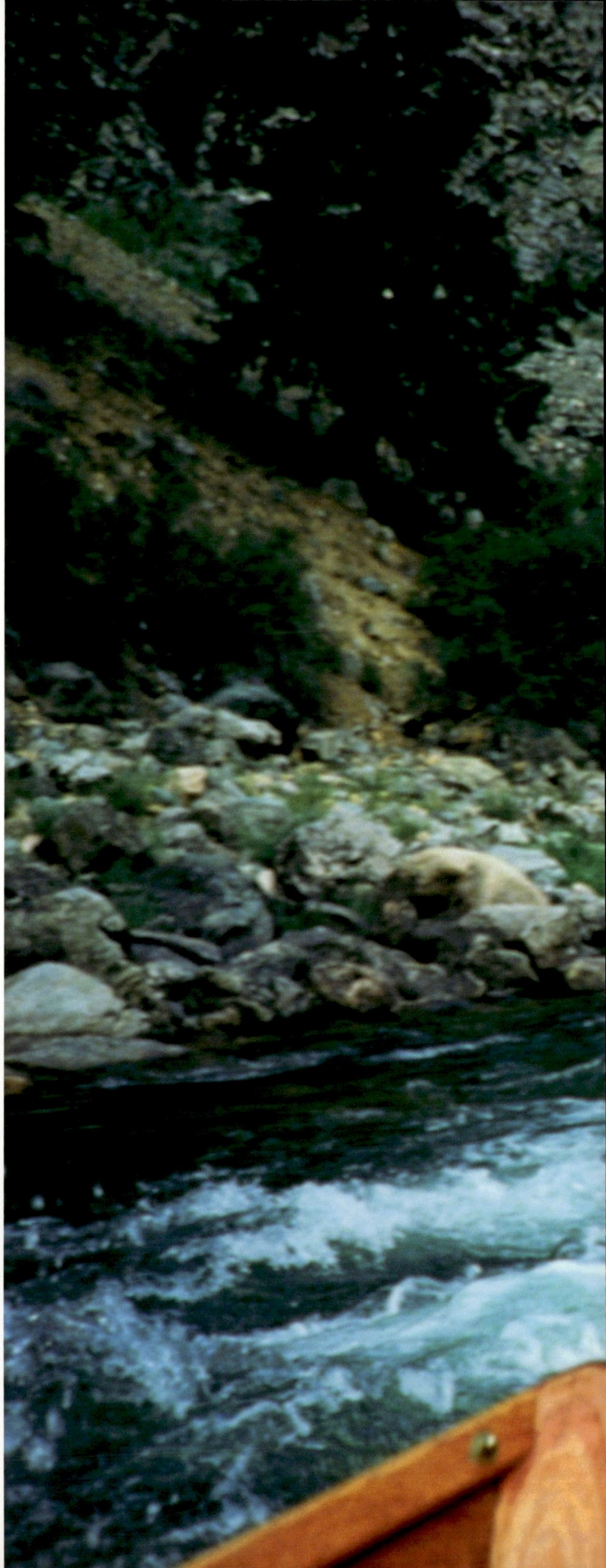

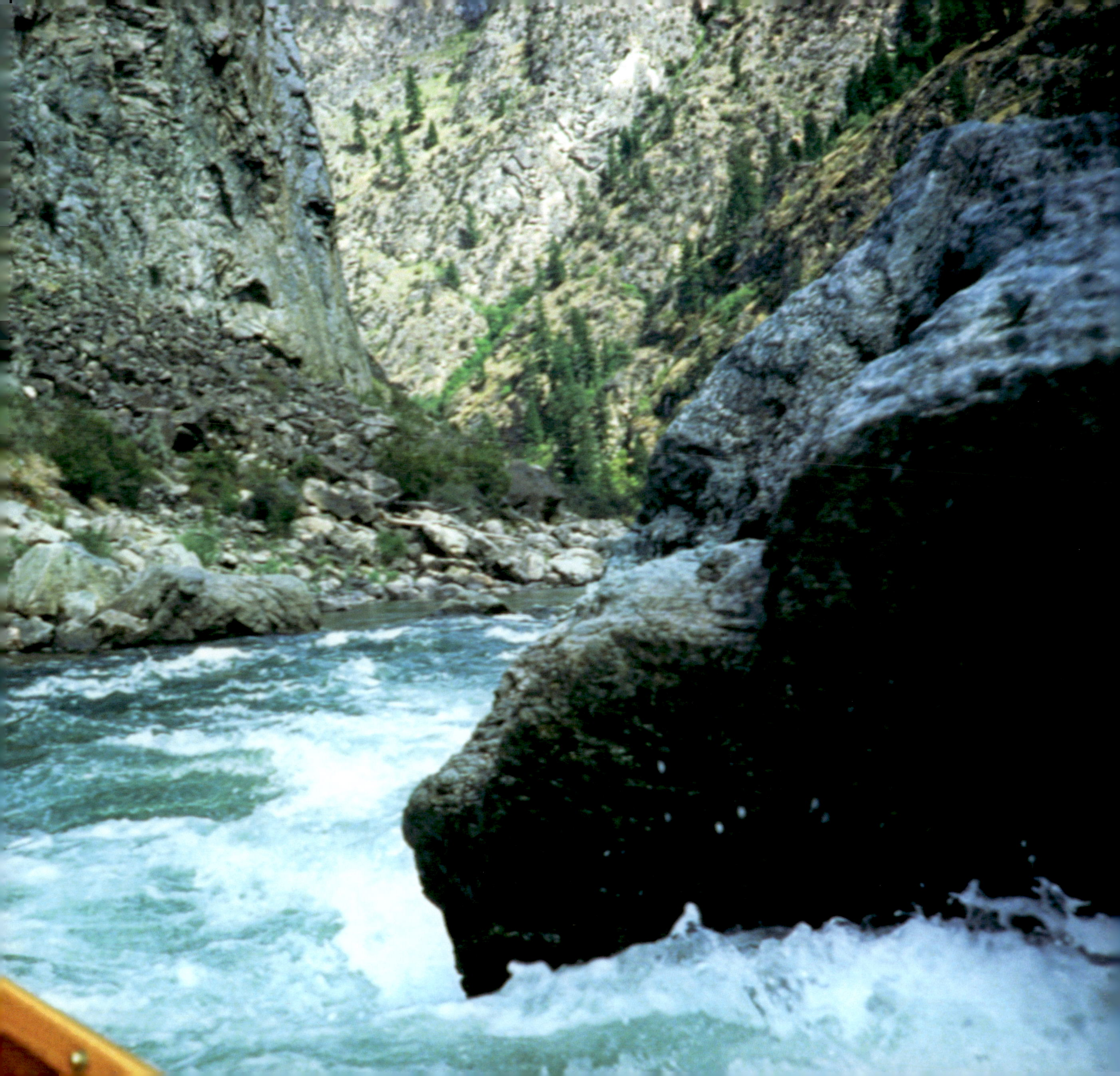

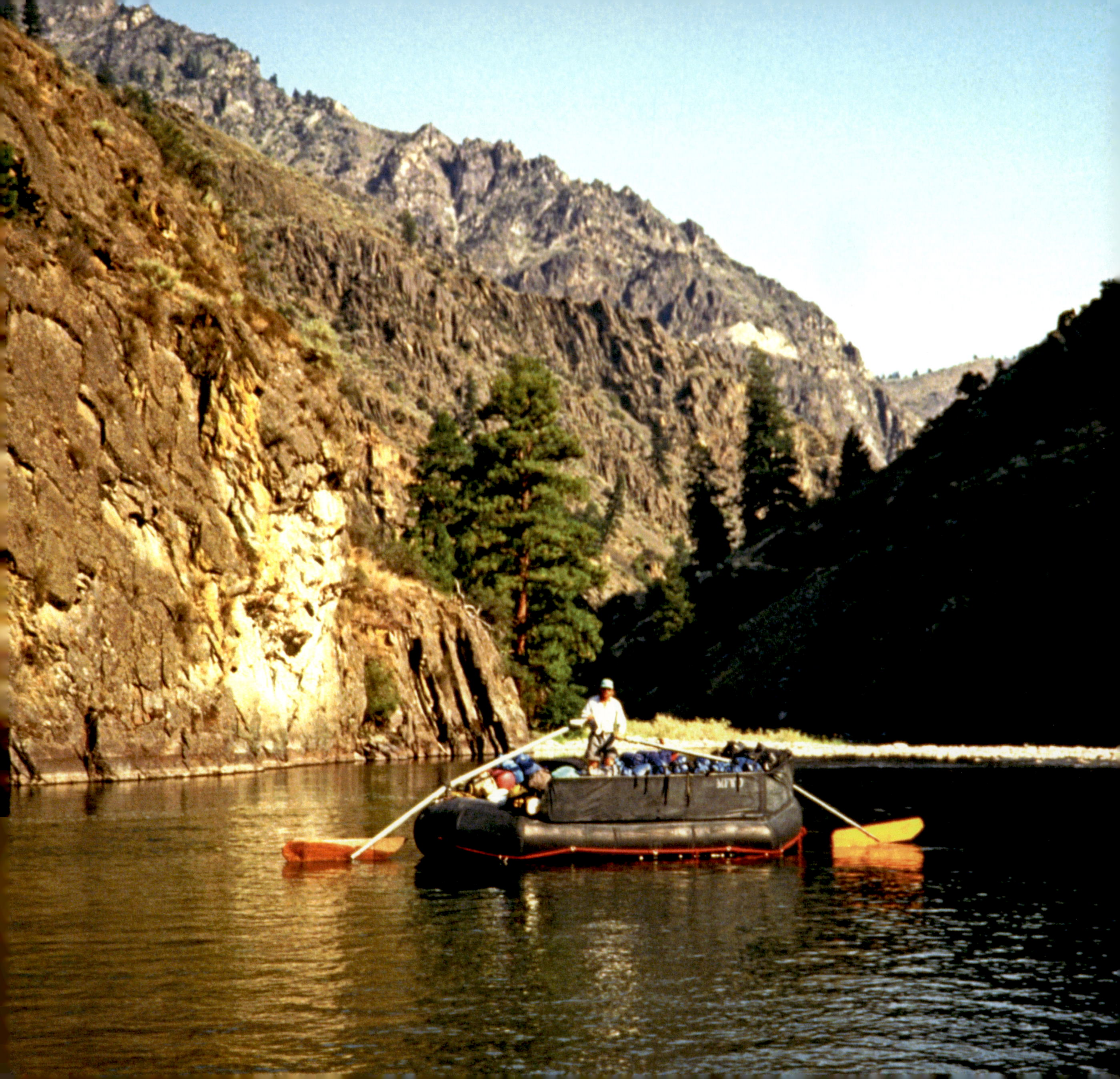

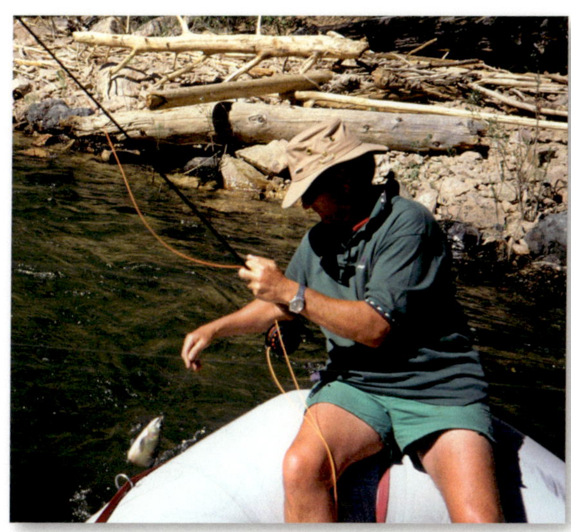

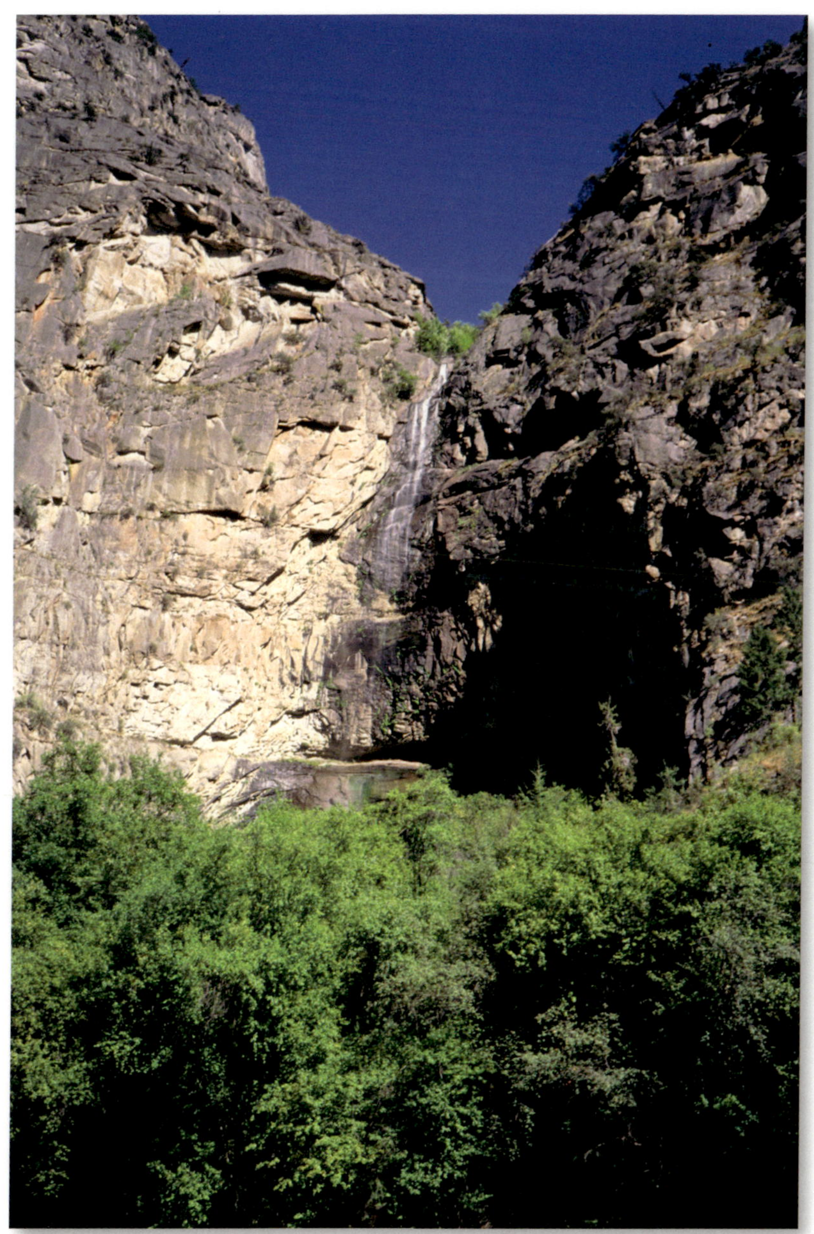

LEFT: Sweep boat almost to camp!

RIGHT: The breathtaking Veil Falls (mile 80)

French Apple Pie (apple
8 Granny Smith apples
cup Flour
mon juice
ustard style vanilla yogurt
TBSP vanilla
cup Brown sugar
cup white sugar
ticks (1 cup) Butter
nnamon 3 shakes
rdomom 2 shakes

top Cru
3 1/2 cups Flo
2 cups sug
1 cup Butt
1 pk cream c

pre cooked cubed
1 can H_2O chestnuts (Drained)
1 can pineapple (Drained)
1/2 can cashews (you can eat the rest)
3-4 carrots chopped
3-4 celery sticks chopped
3/4 ≈ Jar Major Greys chutney
3/4 ≈ cup SOUR cream
3/4 ≈ cup MAYO
curry powder Lots!!
Ginger powder
3/4 can chinese crunchies
salt + pepper

he Devils tooth" cheese cake
RUST
3 TBSP Butter
pk choc wafer cookie crumbs (crush them
illing
2 8 oz pks CREAM cheese
1 tub Ricatta
1/2 cup Floor
6 Eggs
1 cup sugar
1/2 cup whipping cream
1/3 cup sour cream

MEX-avo-Dip (Go
8 avo's peeled + chopped
1 large white onion chopped
2 Tomatoes chopped small
1/2 shredded Iceburg
1 7 oz can Green chili sau
Garlic salt
Pepper
Red pepper
1 1/2 cup grated chedda
1/2 cup MAYO

Granola c̄ Fruit + Yogurt + Rolls + Pig
2 Bags Granola
1 Tub vanilla yogurt
1 Bag Blackberries frozen
1 Bunch Banana's
20 Kiwis
Red + Green Grapes
Milk
Bacon - Mr Dan
Rolls 8 per Dutch
Frost c̄ Baking the pan
can Make the

Veggie Pizza x 2
1) Pre-Made Dough
2) mix Marinara Tom Paste go make sa
3) sauce the dough + yourself
4) slice Eggpl + salt them so they can
mushrooms + eggPlant red pep
Saute garlic cloves

RIVER CUISINE

RECIPES BY GAYLE SELISH

BREAKFAST

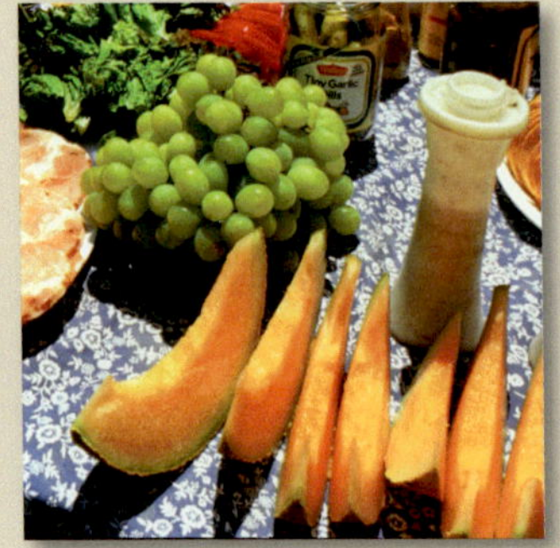

Cinnamon Rolls

1) 6 leaves dough (2 bags)
2) 1 cup butter, melted
3) 1 cup brown sugar
4) walnuts
5) raisens
6) cinnamon
7) nutmeg

Granola, Fruit & Yogurt

1) 2 bags granola
2) 1 tub vanilla yogurt
3) bag black berries (frozen)
4) 1 bunch bananas
5) 20 kiwis
6) red & green grapes
7) milk

River Side Breakfast

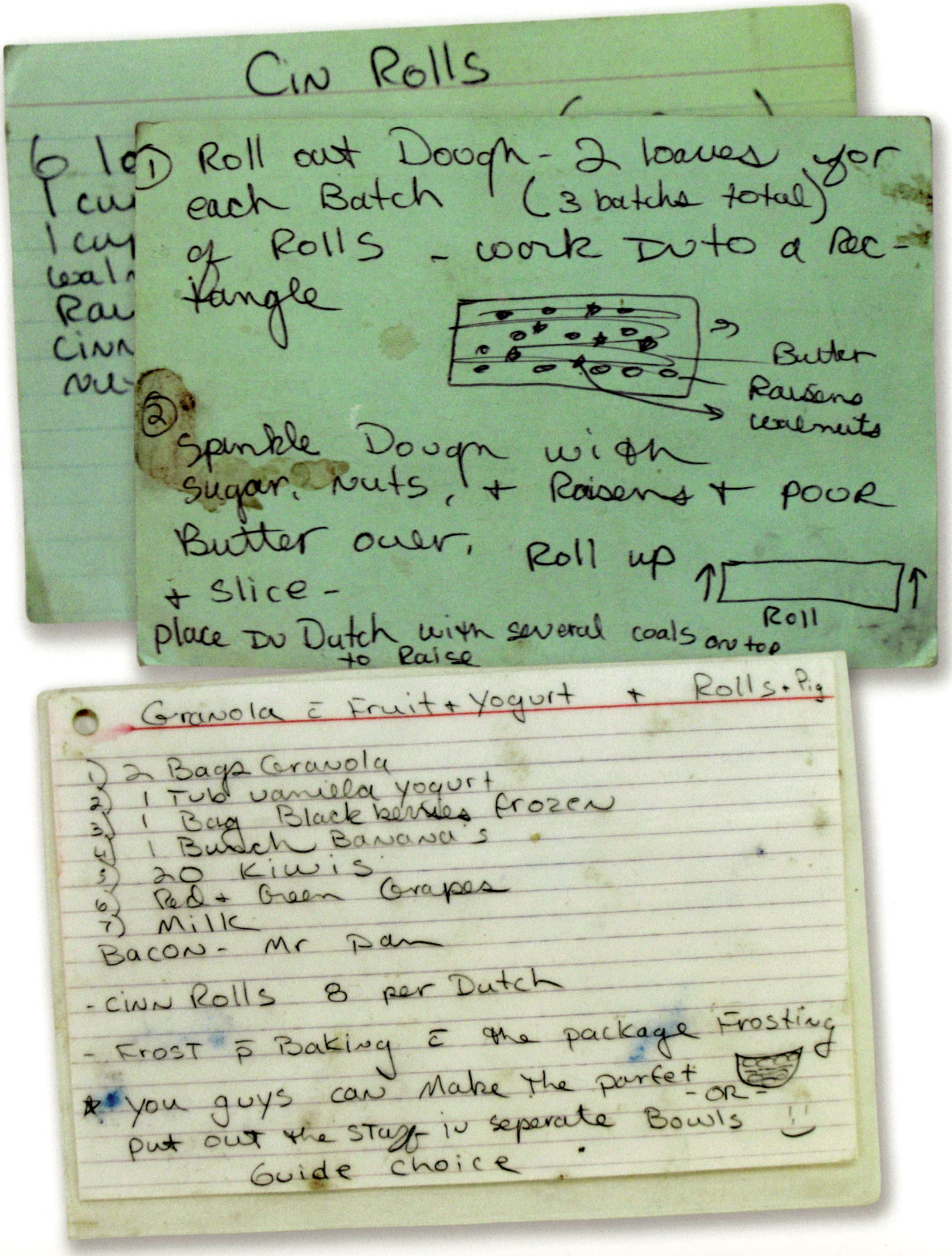

Cin Rolls

6 le
1 cu
1 cu
wal
Rai
CINN
Nu

① Roll out Dough - 2 loaves for each Batch (3 batchs total) of Rolls - work Into a Rec-tangle

Butter
Raisens
walnuts

② Sprinkle Dough with sugar, nuts, + Raisens + poor Butter over. Roll up + slice -

Roll

place In Dutch with several coals on top to Raise

Granola c̄ Fruit + Yogurt + Rolls + Pig

1) 2 Bags Granola
2) 1 Tub vanilla yogurt
3) 1 Bag Blackberries frozen
4) 1 Bunch Banana's
5) 20 Kiwis
6) Red + Green Grapes
7) Milk

Bacon - Mr Dan

- Cinn Rolls 8 per Dutch
- Frost p̄ Baking c̄ the package Frosting

* you guys can make the perfet -OR- put out the stuff in seperate Bowls
Guide choice

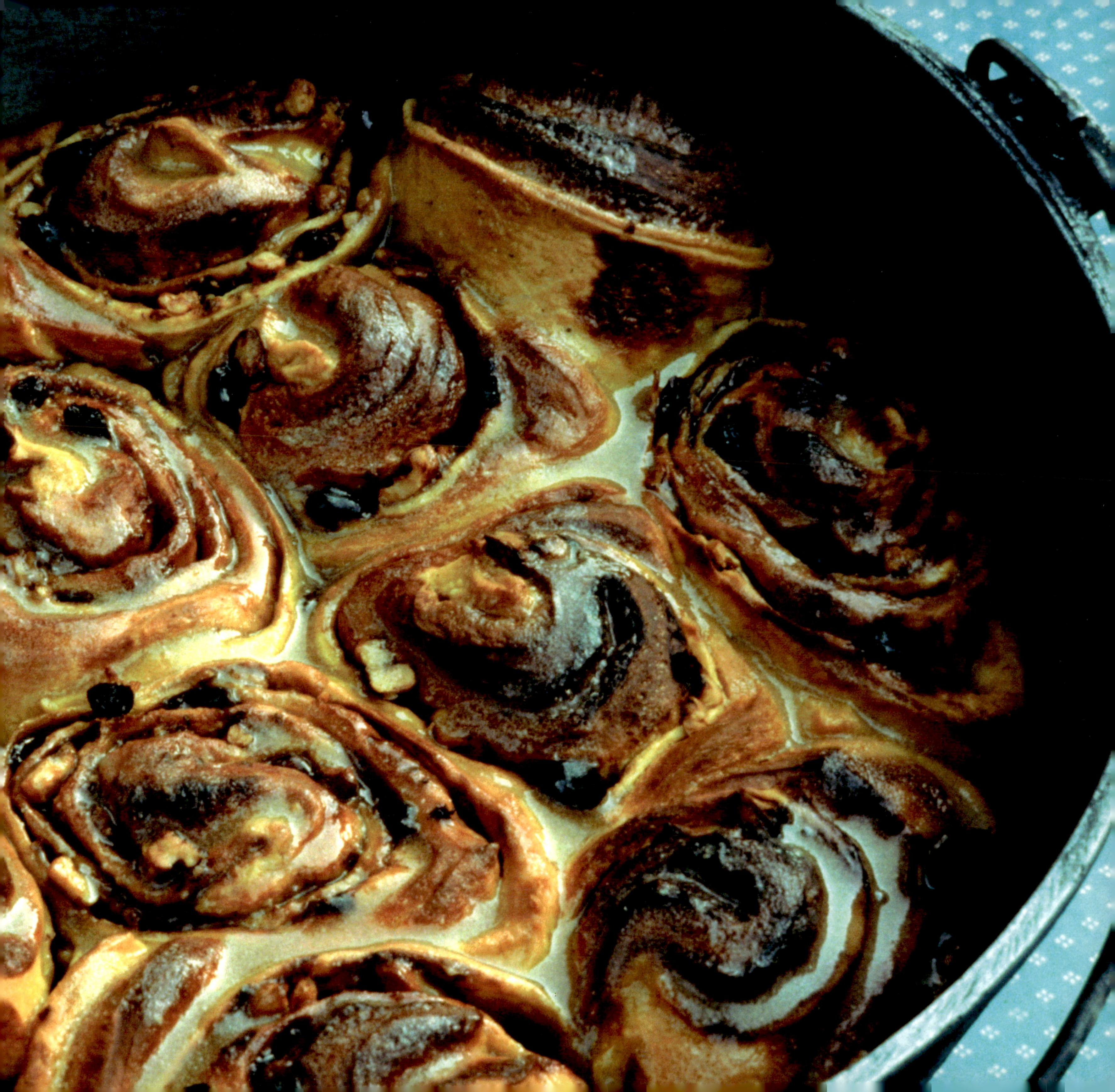

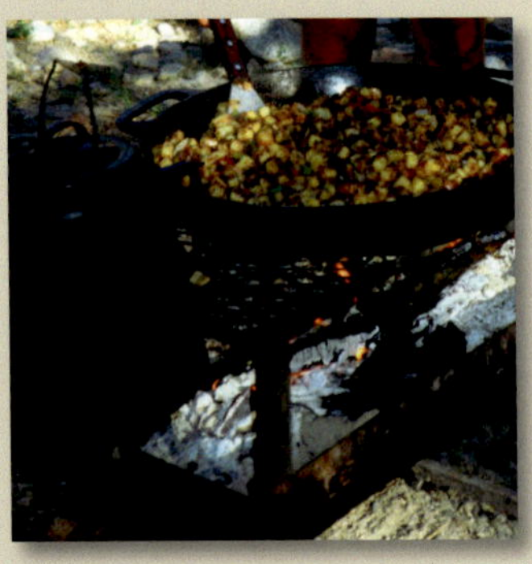

Scalops La Bernese (2 Ovens)

1) 8 lbs. scalops
2) 4 lemons
3) 1 cup flour
4) 6 packs spinach
5) 2 tubs philly
6) 2 tubs Marsapone
7) 4 tomatos
8) 1 cup parmesan
9) 1 bag bread crumbs
10) 1 package chopped prochuitto
11) 2 sticks butter

Crabby Patties

1) Red Rock Crab
2) jar Hain Mayo
3) 1/2 cup finely chopped onion
4) 1/2 cup finely chopped celery
5) bread crumbs
6) 6 eggs
7) 1/3 cup finely chopped garlic
8) salt
9) pepper
10) 3 shakes worchestershire

Dutch Oven Dinners

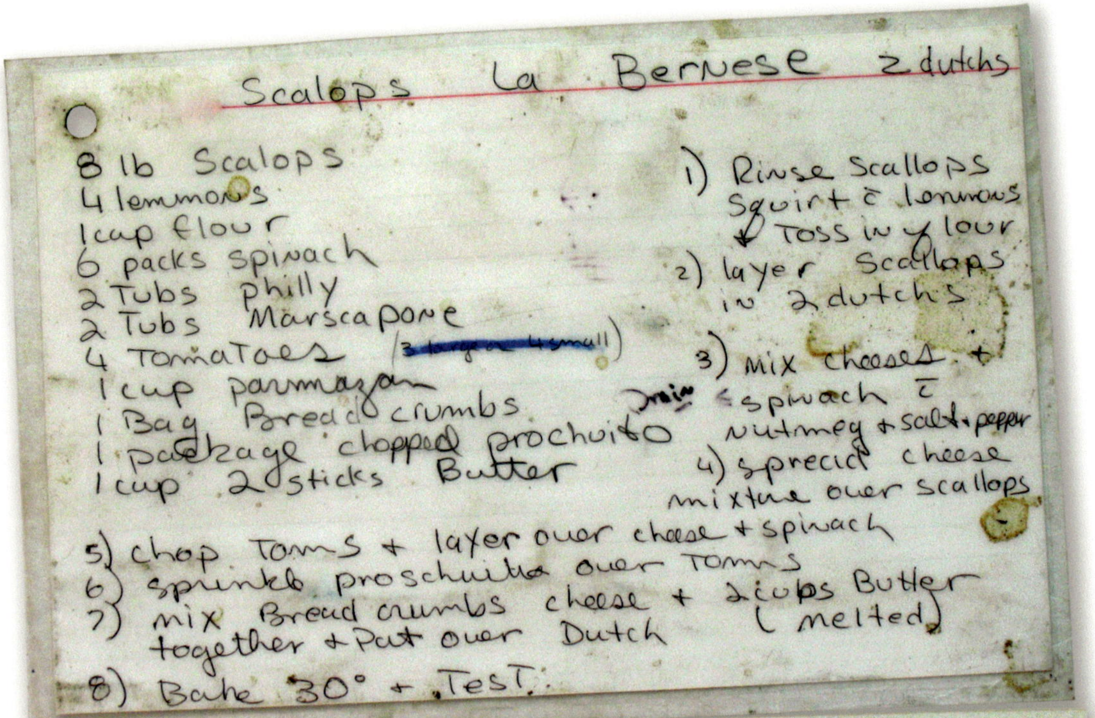

Scalops La Bernese 2 dutchs

8 lb Scalops
4 lemmons
1 cup flour
6 packs spinach
2 Tubs philly
2 Tubs Marscapone
4 Tomatoes ~~(3 large or 4 small)~~
1 cup parmazan
1 Bag Bread crumbs
1 package chopped prochuito (Drain)
1 cup 2 sticks Butter

1) Rinse Scallops Squirt c̄ lemmons & Toss in flour
2) layer Scallops in 2 dutchs
3) Mix cheeses + spinach c̄ nutmeg + salt + pepper
4) spread cheese mixture over scallops
5) chop Toms + layer over cheese + spinach
6) sprinkle proschuitto over Toms
7) mix Bread crumbs cheese + 2 cups Butter (melted) together + Put over Dutch
8) Bake 30° + Test.

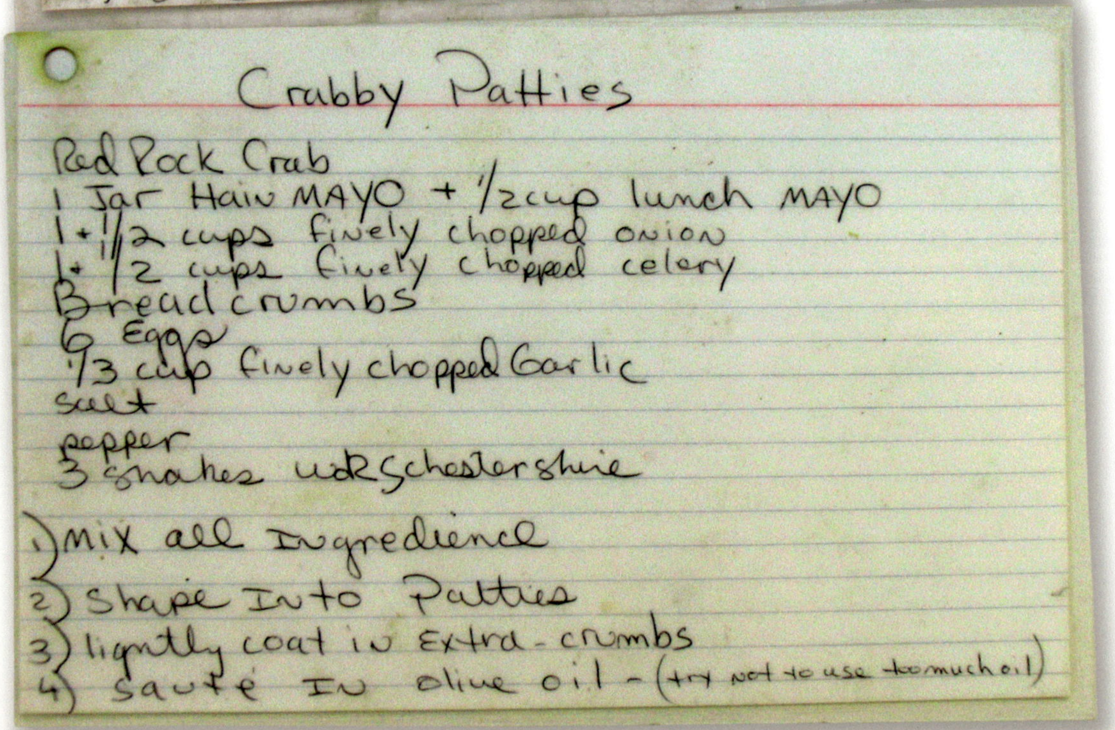

Crabby Patties

Red Rock Crab
1 Jar Hain MAYO + 1/2 cup lunch MAYO
1 + 1/2 cups finely chopped onion
1 + 1/2 cups finely chopped celery
Bread crumbs
6 Eggs
1/3 cup finely chopped Garlic
salt
pepper
3 shakes worschestershire

1) Mix all Ingredience
2) Shape Into Patties
3) lightly coat in Extra-crumbs
4) Sauté In olive oil - (try not to use too much oil)

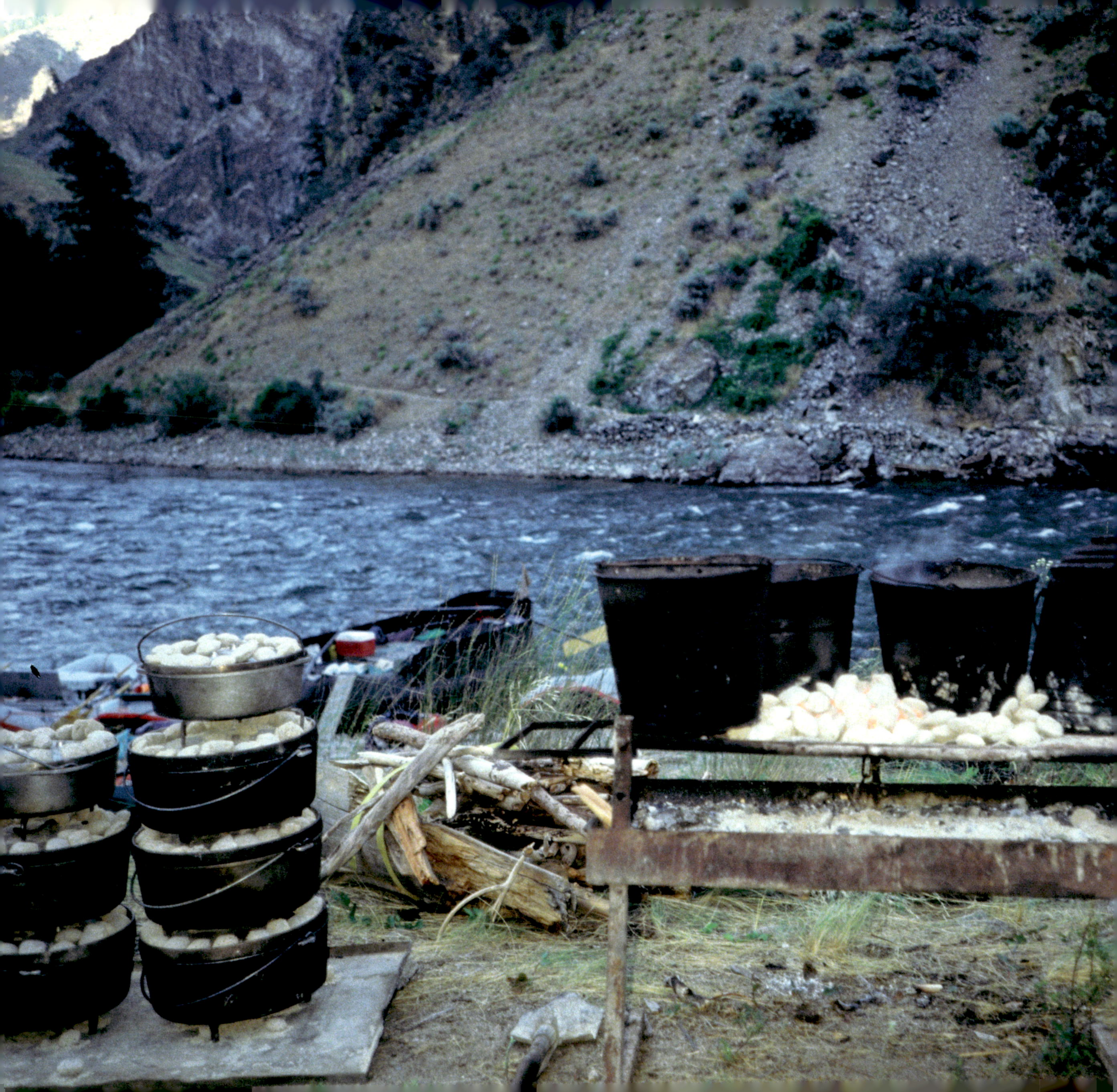

DESSERTS

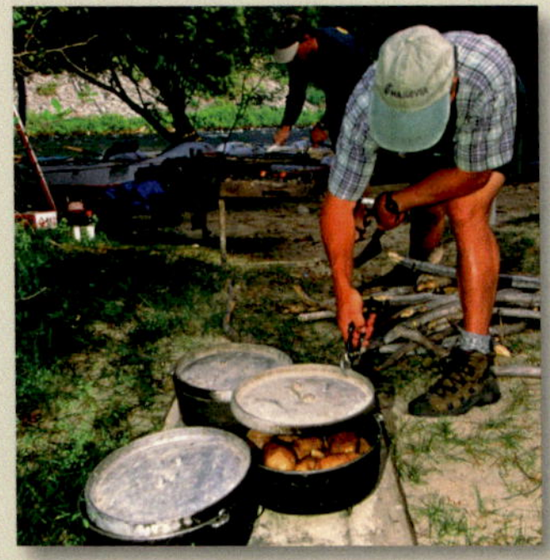

Cherry Dumplings

1) Cherries
2) Pie crust mix (In ziplock)
3) 2 Cups sugar
4) Butter (1 cube)
5) Almond extract (2 tsp)
6) Corn starch (2 tbsp)

"The Devil's Tooth" Cheesecake

CRUST

1) 3 tbsp butter
2) 1 pack wafer cookie crumbs

FILLING

1) Two 8oz packs cream cheese
2) 1 tub ricatta
3) 1/2 cup flour
4) 6 eggs
5) 1 cup sugar
6) 1/2 cup whipping cream
7) 1/3 cup sour cream
8) vanilla extract
9) almond extract
10) 12 oz chocolate chips

Delectable Desserts

Cherry Dumplings

Dumplings

cherries
pie crust mix in Ziplock
Sugar - 2 cups
Butter 1 cube cut in little chunks
almond Extract - 2TSP
CORN STarch - 2 TABLESPOONS 1/2

1) PaT the Crusts into 2 Dutches.
2) pour cherries in Bowl + cover with the sugar, butter, almond, corn starch + let sit 15 min. - pour into crusts.
3) make Dumplings with the Puff pastry - any shape you want. Roll in (nothing Phallic please) sugar + cinnamon + press into ch… Bake 30 min

"The Devils tooth" cheese cake

CRUST
3 TB…
1 pk…
Fillin…
2 8…
1 tub…
1/2 c…
6 E…
1 cu…
1/2 cu…
1/3 c…
van…
alm…
12…

[CRUST]
1) crush cookies IN Ziplock pour INTO greased 10" Dutch
2) melt the 3 TBSP Butt + mix in crumbs press crumbs to form crust (up the sides too.)

[Filling]
1) melt choc chips + 2 TSPB Butt over STOVE OVER very Low heat (chocolate Burns Easily) add whipping cream add almond Extract 1+1/2 TSP set aside
2) IN large Bowl mix together:
cream cheese (2)
Ricatta (1 tub)
Flour (1/2 cup)
Sour Cream (1/3 cup)
eggs (6)
Sugar (1 cup)
Vanilla 1 1/2 tsp
mix very well

[assemble]
1) add 1/3 of the vanilla Batter INTO the chocolate Batter - mix well + pour INTO CRUST.
2) pour Rest of vanilla Batter into dutch on top of chocolate (Don't stir it)
3) Bake for at least 1° the top should crack + it should not jiggle :) cool.

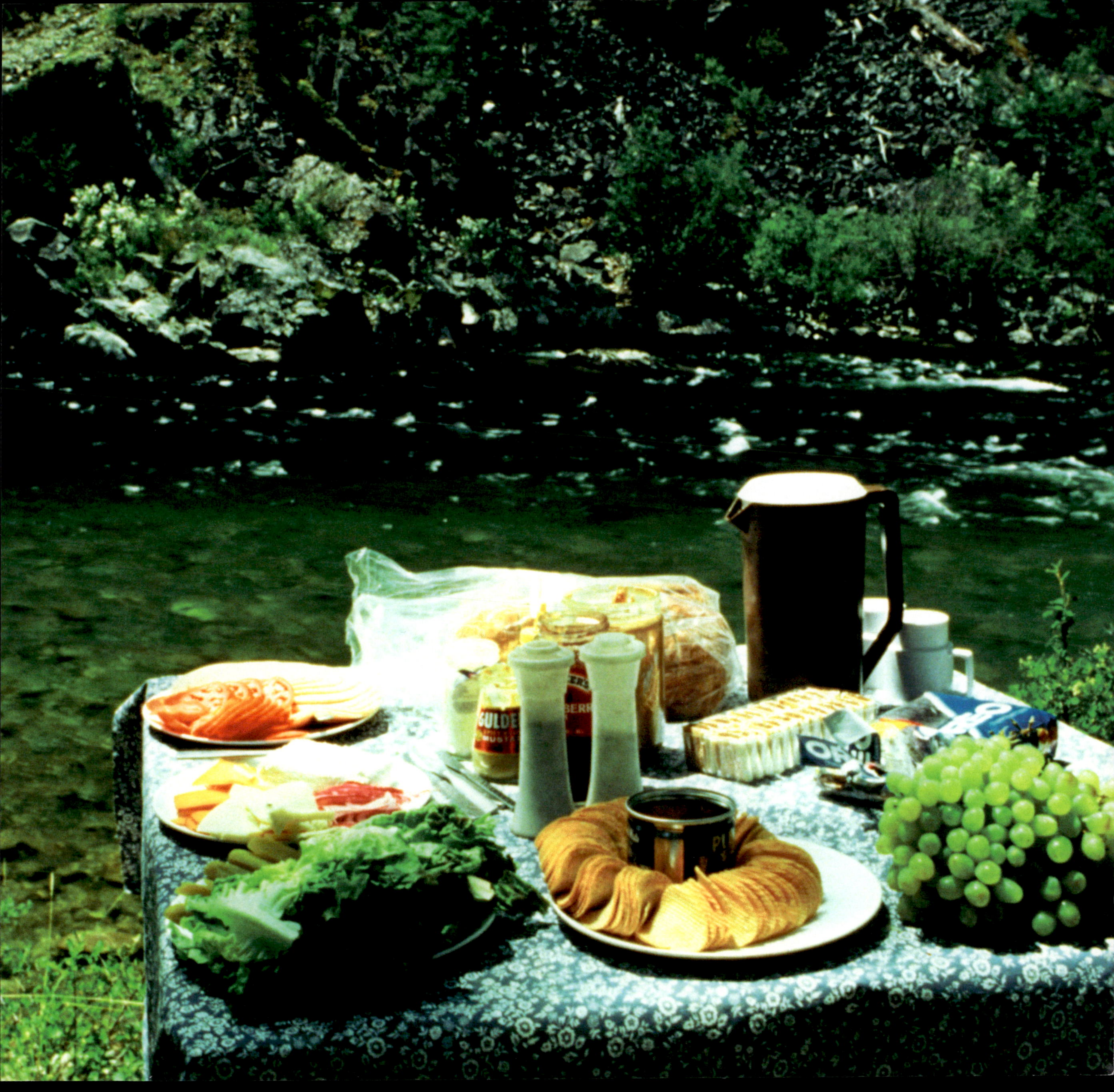

Acknowledgements:

This book has been a long time in the making. Without my friend Kurt Selish, veteran river guide and outfitter, and his wife Gayle, this book would not have been possible. In addition, several photographers all of whom are more talented than the author graciously provided additional photos for the book. They include (in alphabetical order) Cindy Jimmerson, Ken Morrish, Brian O'Keefe, Kurt Selish, Bill Sheppard, Keenan Ward, Jack Williams, and Angel Wynn.

Over the years, the author has had the privilege of knowing a number of people who possess a deep appreciation for the preservation of wild rivers and wild trout. In one way or another, they have all had an impact on the author in their own unique way. A special thanks to Frank Amato, Mark Bachman, Bud Beamer, Fred Boyle, Frank Cammack, Rod Englert, Jerry Fletcher, Lynn Guenther, Rick Haeffle, Jim Hall, Dave Helfrich, John Huffman, Dave Hughs, Loren Irving, Dar Isensee, Cindy Jimmerson, Randall Kaufman, Ted Leeson, Bill Lerch, Jack Mauer, George Mendenhall, Ron Nelson, Brian O'Keefe, Jeff Pampush, Jim Quinn, Dan Re, Eric Rector, Terry Ring, Royal and Liz Robbins, Jim Rozewski, Jim Schollmeyer, John Smerglio, Travis Smith and Jim Van Loan.

Finally, and most importantly, thanks to Jodie, Brandon, Erin and Mary Bischof for sharing many wonderful summers on the Middle Fork.

About the Author:

Bruce Bischof of Bend, Oregon has been floating western rivers most of his adult life. He is a licensed guide on the Middle Fork where he has taken several thousand photos over a 20 year period.

747 SW Mill View Way
Bend, Oregon 97702
Ph:541.389.1292 ▪ FAX:541.389.0270
bruce@middleforkriver.net
www.middleforkriver.net

International Standard Book Number: ISBN 0-9716040-3-7

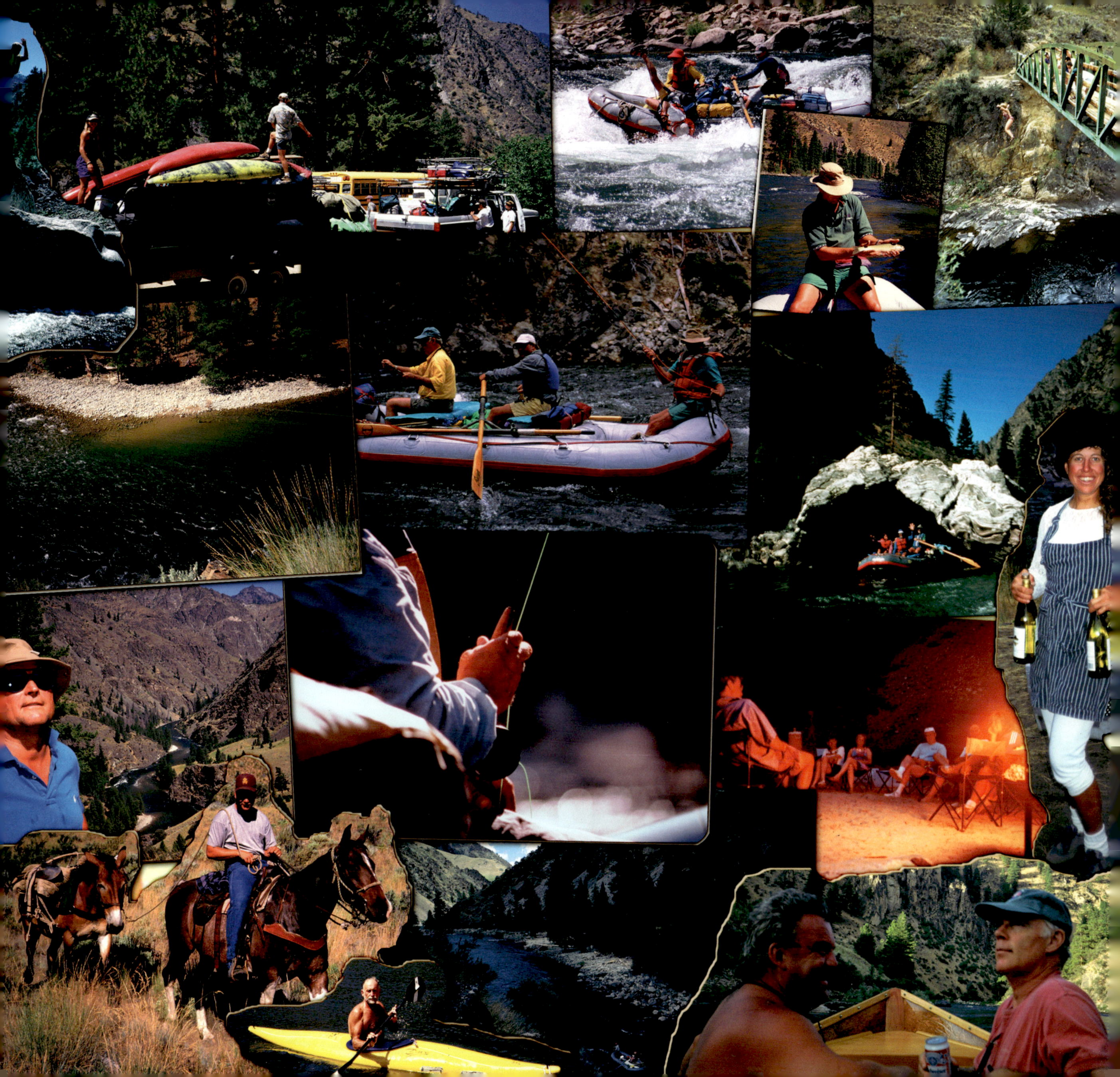

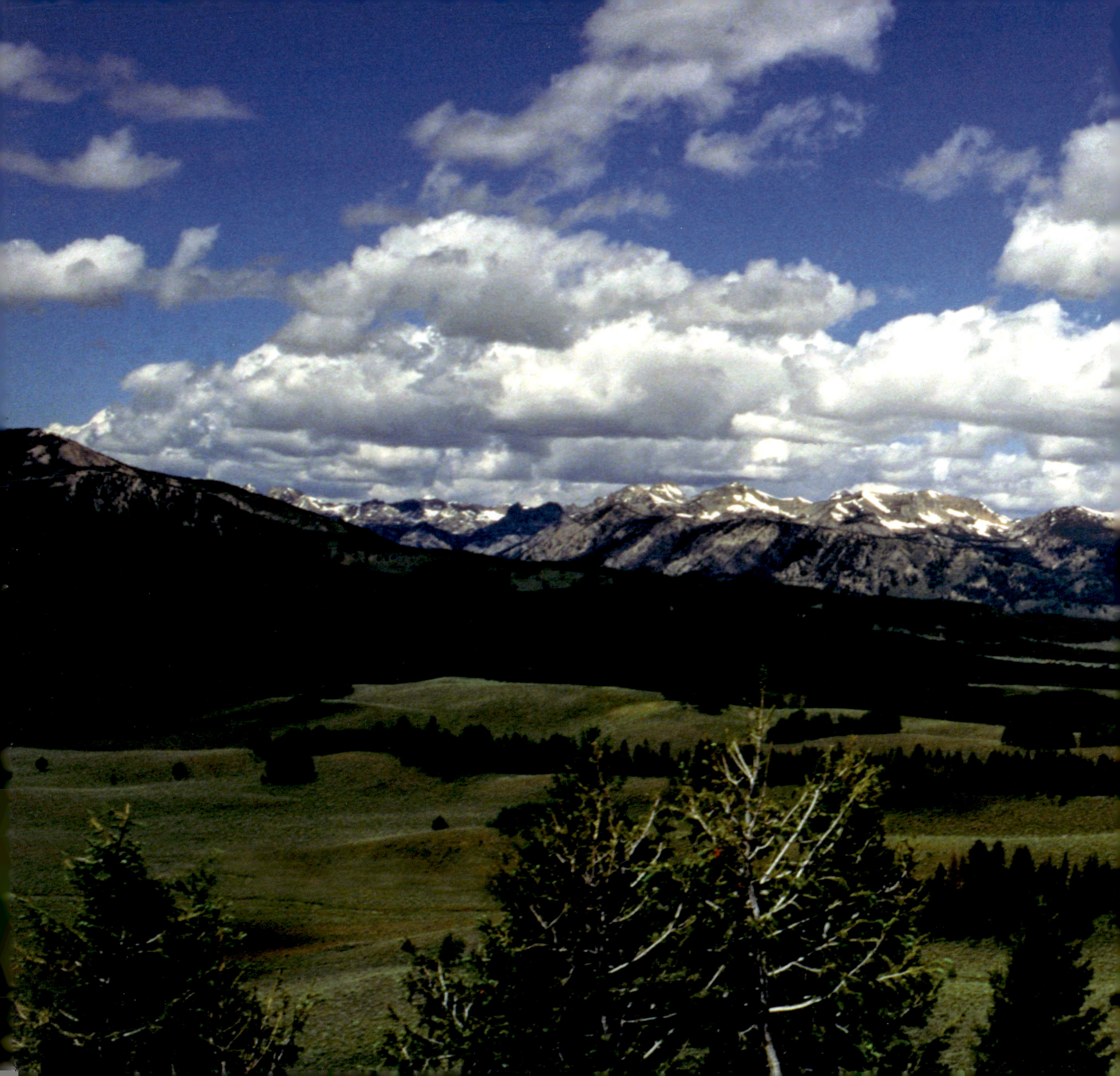